D1168644

NOW
that You're a
DEACON

NOW
that You're a
DEACON

HOWARD B. FOSHEE

BROADMAN
& HOLMAN
PUBLISHERS

Nashville, Tennessee

Library of Congress Catalog Card Number: 74-79488
Dewey Decimal Classification: 262
Printed in the United States of America

99 00 01   8 7 6

TO PAST AND PRESENT staff members of the Church Administration Department, Sunday School Board of the Southern Baptist Convention, who have labored so diligently in developing concepts and approaches for more effective deacon ministry, many of which appear in this book.

CONTENTS

1
Understand Your Work as a Deacon

Now that you are a deacon, there is great work for you to do. I recall reading a newspaper article about Dr. John Tyndall, the renowned British scientist who excelled in molecular physics. Someone asked Dr. Tyndall who had been of the greatest influence on his life. He answered quickly that the person of greatest influence had been an old friend who had lived with him through the years as a servant. Dr. Tyndall said, "Each morning my friend would knock on my bedroom door and call out: 'It is 7:00 o'clock, sir. Get up! You have great work to do today!'"

The same is true for you as a new deacon. You have great work to do today. I hope that you feel God's energy flowing through you. My wish for you is that you experience a sense of divine purpose as did Jesus when he said, "I must be about my Father's business." And feel the thrill of service as Paul when he said, "For this day was I born!" You can find no happier person than the individual who is busy for the Master, using his gifts in Christian service. One of nature's masterpieces truly is the man absorbed in his work and loving every minute of it.

So much depends on you! Hurt abounds in this world

and cries out for spiritual healing. Aching souls reach out for a caring, listening, compassionate friend. Though spoken to his weary troops, the words of George Washington seem to present a special challenge for deacons: "The fate of unborn millions may now depend, under God, upon the conduct and courage of this army. Our country's honor calls upon us for vigorous and manly exertion, and if we now shamefully fail, we shall become infamous to the whole world. Let every good soldier be silent and attentive; wait for orders, and reserve his fire until he is sure of doing execution."

The prayer of deacons today could well be that found on the epitaph of Winifred Holtby, the English novelist.

> God give me work
> Till my life shall end,
> And life
> Till my work is done.

Deacons Originated in New Testament Times

The heritage of deacon service goes back to New Testament times. Pastors and deacons have served as brothers in ministry through the centuries. Longevity of service does not give deacons any special position or power, but it does provide an extra dimension of continuity that motivates for greater service. People like to be involved with the beginning of movements. Enjoyment comes from being a charter member or belonging to a group that has a direct link with the past. Deacons have such a link with the past and can trace their ministry as far back as the early churches.

New Testament deacons have a noble heritage. But even more important they have a place of worthy purpose in both the present and the future, serving Christ as did "the seven" described in the Acts 6 account of the first church in Jerusalem.

Someone told me about a pastor who was attending the weekly meeting of his civic club. The presiding officer was acknowledging fellow businessmen whose firms had served continuously through the years. One member was recognized whose business had originated more than fifty years before. Another man indicated that he belonged to a firm that had operated for almost one hundred years. The presiding officer then asked, "Is there anyone else here whose organization has served more than one hundred years?" The pastor rose and good-naturedly answered, "I serve as pastor of an organization that has existed for almost two thousand years." Today's deacon might well have made this comment regarding his deacon heritage.

Heritage adds dimension to your deacon service, but it does not provide special privilege or authority. Spiritual needs cry out for deacons to be stalwart disciples on Christian mission. Prepare yourself for encounter in Christ's name. Develop skills and motivation to meet crushing spiritual needs for today and tomorrow.

Deacon Work Originated to Meet Spiritual Needs

As the early church in Jerusalem grew rapidly, there arose a "murmuring" among some of the members. The misunderstanding arose between Jewish Christians who continued to follow ancient Hebrew traditions and other Jewish Christians who had accepted the language and social customs of Greece and Rome. The actual misunderstanding developed over the methods used for administering the daily food distribution to their Jewish widows. The incident, as recorded in Acts 6, was only an outward symptom of a deeper problem. The major problem was a potential break in Christian fellowship.

The devil still uses this same devastating strategy today. He works stealthily, seeking to bring about discontent and murmuring among Christians.

The Acts 6 account does not use the word "deacon" but rather refers to "the seven." It is generally agreed that "deacon" soon evolved from the precedent set by "the seven."

The Holy Spirit led the Jerusalem congregation to choose these seven men of proven spiritual maturity to aid in resolving a fellowship problem. These Christian leaders were chosen and then ordained following the ancient Hebrew custom of laying on of hands as an expression of confidence and affirmation.

This account of "the seven" is the first organized use of church members to help the young church achieve its divine mission. "The seven" were obviously successful in resolving the fellowship problem because the Scriptures indicate that "the word of God increased; and the number of disciples multiplied in Jerusalem greatly; and a great company of the priests were obedient to the faith" (Acts 6:7).

The ministry of the deacon grew rapidly in the early churches, for the Scriptures show that Paul's greetings to the churches often had references to the deacons.

In 1 Timothy 3, Paul set forth the spiritual qualifications for both the deacon and his wife.

After the second century A.D., the Roman church began to form its elaborate hierarchical structure. The deacons gradually became a part of the clergy. It was not until the Reformation that the deacon was again viewed as a lay leader rather than a member of the clergy.

As Baptist churches were established in America during the eighteenth and nineteenth centuries, deacons played a significant leadership role in the life of these churches. Being servants of the church, as the very word "deacon" implies, they served wherever there was a need. Because the churches were small and leaders were few, deacons were called on to provide significant leadership responsibilities. In many churches the business matters were handled totally by the deacons. The unfortunate term "board of deacons" arose. This phrase, however, is foreign to the way Baptists should work together under the leadership of the Holy Spirit. A Baptist congregation makes corporate decisions as each member seeks to vote his conviction under the leadership of the Lord.

Deacon Otis Bardwell shared the following comment in a deacon ordination sermon in his church.* "A person is not made a deacon just for the honor, although it is an honor beyond most of the things that can come to a man's life. The deacon is set apart to serve; he is committed to serve God and his fellowman. As a

*This illustration and others indicated by an asterisk throughout the book are from articles in *The Deacon*, a magazine published quarterly by The Sunday School Board of the Southern Baptist Convention.

new deacon, you must understand that you have not been elected to an 'official board' to exercise authority in the life of the church. The office of deacon is not an office of authority but one of service. A man who agrees to serve as a deacon in a New Testament church agrees to be an example, to the limit of God's enduement, in all the life of the church. He is to be an example in spirit, love, devotion, and loyalty."

Deacons Have a Worthy Purpose

I like to be with people who are captivated by a special purpose in life. There is something electric about a person who is on a worthy mission.

I am inspired by memory of the life and work of Dr. J. M. Frost, the first leader of the Sunday School Board of the Southern Baptist Convention, Nashville, Tennessee. Dr. Frost breathed his spirit into this great institution as he led it during difficult early days. His one overriding purpose in life was to provide resources for Bible study. There is in the lobby of one of the Sunday School Board buildings a plaque placed in memory of Dr. Frost with this simple inscription.

> DIVINELY LED
> HIS FAITH CONCEIVED IT
> HIS GENIUS PLANNED IT
> HIS COURAGE BUILT IT.

These words could well express the tribute due deacons who have served Christ well through the centuries.

The Holy Spirit led in the establishment of deacon service. The original purpose was significant—to preserve the spiritual fellowship of his church.

How do deacons serve *today?* What is the ministry of the deacon?

Deacons serve as persons who care. The world is filled with the muted cries of persons who hurt. People are lonely, lost, confused. Having no foundation on which to stand and no North Star by which to set their life's compass, many persons are like derelict ships floating aimlessly at sea. Deacons have a place of service today that is unparalleled in Christian history.

I was enriched and strengthened by what pastor David R. Young said as he told of his first encounter with a deacon who cared.* The lasting influence of this deacon enabled this pastor to develop an appreciation and fellowship with deacons that have lasted through the years. He said: "At the first meeting of the deacons I attended, this deacon spoke of the sick people in the community. Then he reminded us that there were some young parents in the community and told us of a new baby who had just been born. He noted some new residents in the community. He spoke of an elderly person who had appreciated a visit. He reminded us of our financial needs as a church.

"Then, he looked at every person in that group, including me, and asked us all about our lives, our own needs. One father revealed his agony over a rebellious daughter. One man was facing surgery. I had just faced a financial crisis.

"I have never forgotten how this deacon expressed a fatherly interest in our congregation and a brotherly interest in his fellow deacons. He was an example of what a deacon is called to be and do. Deacons are set apart to minister to the members of a congregation. He serves as an undershepherd ever alert to care for the well-being of the flock."

Deacons Should Organize for Ministry

Deacon organization whould be simple and directed toward getting their basic work done. When organization is overly complex, work is usually impeded rather than strengthened.

In years past, deacons often organized their work by committees since they primarily performed administrative work. In today's churches, when most committees are church committees, deacons are organizing in a different manner in order to better implement their spiritual ministry to families.

Pastor Young, seeking to interpret to church members the organized ministry of the deacons, had this to say in an ordination sermon.*

"Deacons are shepherds; they walk with us along the journey of life. When there are mountain peaks of joy and happiness, when there are valleys of the shadows of death, we are not alone. God is walking with us, getting through to us with his love—yes, in the lives of good shepherds like these deacons. Thank God for them.

"Each family in this congregation will have one person who is specifically set apart to serve that family. He will visit you; he will get acquainted with your children; he'll know when your child goes to kindergarten or college; he'll know when you have a birthday. He is your Christian friend, your shepherd. He will give you his telephone number at work, and at home he will be as near to you as your telephone. So, will you talk with him? Will you call on him? He is making a covenant with you and your family to be your servant. However, your deacon will need your encouragement if he is to do his job well."

This pastor was helping his people to understand how their deacons were seeking to minister to church families. The deacons were working closely with the pastor, as undershepherds of the flock.

One channel of deacon service is the Deacon Family Ministry Plan. This is a pattern of organization designed to reach every family in the church by regular visitation in homes. Church families are grouped in some systematic ways and assigned to deacons who serve as shepherds of their smaller flock. Each deacon is responsible for the pastoral care of twelve to fifteen families.

The chairman of deacons serves as general director of the Deacon Family Ministry Plan. He, of course, fulfills his other duties required of a chairman. His primary responsibility, however, is to serve as chairman of the Deacon Family Ministry Plan. This plan is not just a terminal project but serves as the pattern for organizing the entire deacon body. Through the Deacon Family Ministry Plan, deacons are able to implement their responsibilities for proclaiming the gospel, caring for members of the church fellowship, assisting the church to build and maintain a Christian fellowship, and serving as exemplar Christian leaders in the church and community.

Through such an organized ministry, individual families are strengthened, the entire church receives benefit of deacon ministry, and church fellowship is enhanced.

Certainly, there are alternate patterns by which the Deacon Family Ministry Plan can be organized to meet the unique needs in your church. The basic plan, however, calls for each deacon to be assigned twelve to fifteen families. Families might be grouped either alphabetically or geographically, according to your specific needs. If your church serves a college campus or apartment complex, one deacon might be given responsibility for church members in one dormitory or apartment building.

The primary purpose of the Deacon Family Ministry Plan is to maintain regular contact with church members so that encouragement, support, and nurture is provided. Deacons should visit in the home at intervals to maintain a contact from the church. In times of crisis each deacon seeks to provide Christian concern and ministry. He remains alert at all times for persons who are not Christians. Often, as he visits in homes he will discover a family member or family relative who needs a Christian witness. Like a sensitive radar, each deacon should ever be tuned to pick up signals that report problems, spiritual needs, or potential breaks in the church fellowship.

More information regarding this plan of organization is given in the Program Help pamphlet *The Deacon Family Ministry Plan,* the book *The Ministry of the Deacon* by Howard B. Foshee, and *The Deacon Tapes* (3 cassette tapes) by Treadway and Foshee. (See "List of Resources" at the end of the book.)

Life Will Be Enriched by Your Deacon Ministry

Serving as a deacon in ministry will enrich the lives of those you serve. And your own spiritual strength will be renewed through service to others.

You may be asking: "Can I perform this type of deacon ministry? Do I have the skills and the time? Will my attempts at deacon ministry be accepted? Can I—will I—have opportunity to learn new skills to help me perform my deacon work in an acceptable manner?"

Deacons have an opportunity for ministry that is unique. A deacon, in fact, has some advantages going for him that even his pastor does not possess. Elton Trueblood, noted professor and writer says: "First, the layman does not have to bear the stigma of being a clergyman. The clergyman is often expected to be a 'good' person. He is supposed to visit the sick, to care for people. After all, 'this is what he is paid to do.' Whereas, the layman is free from any of these expectations and, thus, his presence is often taken more seriously. Second, the layman is often closer to common life. He is already in the factory, the bank, the office, the school, and, thus, does not have to gain entrance from the outside. Third, the lay minister has a certain freshness. Often the training of the clergymen blinds him to possible new ways of doing and thinking, whereas the layman can bring a freshness to the task." [1]

What about the time required? The old limerick comes to mind when you dig around looking for just a few minutes of available time.

---

[1] *Your Other Vocation* (New York: Harper and Brothers, 1952) pp. 41-42.

> Breathes there a man with soul so dead
> Who never to himself hath said
> Just how thin can one guy get spread?

But remember your priorities! What is important in your life? What are you busy about?

Usually, God looks for the busy man when he wants a big job done. He does not turn to the lazy. The man for a priority job is already at work!

Abraham and David were watching over their flocks.

Andrew and Peter were busy casting out fishing nets.

Matthew worked full time at tax collection.

William Carey had a backlog of shoes to mend.

Bill Wallace had a medical practice.

Luke, himself a busy physician, records, "He that is faithful in that which is least is faithful also in much" (Luke 16:10).

As a teenager my life was shaped by the book *I Dare You* by William Danforth. Catherine Bates, long-time Baptist educator, gave me the book while she served as a summer educational worker in my home church. The book grabbed me and shook my life with the challenge to live a disciplined Christian life in service to God and fellowman. The writer drove home his challenge with a loving "I dare you!"

Now—I dare you to make your term of deacon service a period of personal spiritual growth and involvement in Christian service.

Theodore Roosevelt expressed well the thrill of new service in saying, "Far better is it to dare mighty things, to win glorious triumphs, even though checkered by failure, than to take ranks with those poor spirits who neither enjoy much nor suffer much, because they live in the gray twilight that knows not victory nor defeat."

You will never be the same again after joining the battle. Oliver Wendell Holmes said, "A man's mind, stretched by a new idea, can never go back to its original dimension." Get involved in deacon service! Become a partner with your pastor in ministry!

I dare you to join with Hudson Taylor, founder of the pioneer China Inland Mission, whose stated life purpose was:

> Be God's Man
> In God's Place
> Doing God's Work
> In God's Way.

2
Serve as Partner
with Your Pastor

Now that you are a deacon, you have become a partner in Christian service with your pastor. God in his divine wisdom established the offices of pastor and deacon. Pastor and deacons share a divine responsibility to proclaim the gospel to believers and unbelievers, provide care for church members and other persons of the community, build and maintain church fellowship, and provide Christian leadership in order to help their church attain its spiritual mission.

You are a co-laborer—a partner with your pastor in God's work.

I was impressed by some insights that Pastor Roger Lovette once shared regarding the partnership of Paul and Timothy.° Lovette said: "While studying the book of Philippians, I was struck by the opening verse: 'Paul and Timothy, servants of Christ Jesus, to all the saints in Christ Jesus who are at Philippi' (Phil. 1:1, RSV).

"Why would Paul, who wrote this letter, give Timothy—a young, inexperienced preacher—credit for the writing, too? Why is it that both received 'equal time' at the beginning of this letter?

"As I dug into the background of this relationship, I discovered something quite interesting. Timothy was with Paul at this writing in Rome. The young preacher had been with him in Corinth when he scratched out the first and second letters to the Thessalonians. He was in Ephesus when Paul wrote 1 Corinthians and in Macedonia when 2 Corinthians had been written. Timothy, the young man, had been with Paul when the Philippian church was founded.

"Something had happened to Paul, perhaps the hard way. He had learned to lean on this young man, Timothy.

"What I see in this simple introductory verse is a basic principle for every church. If any congregation is to be effective in its ministry, there must be a Paul and a Timothy at the heart of things.

"It takes Paul and Timothy to assume responsibility, but I also think there must be a Paul and a Timothy to shoulder the emotional load of one another.

"All of us need the emotional support that comes from somebody else. The pastor ought to find that support from his deacons and his people; the people ought to find that support from their deacons and pastor and others in the fellowship.

"I think that first verse in Philippians provides us with a clue to it all. 'Paul and Timothy, servants of Christ Jesus.' Deacons are called 'servants' in the New Testament.

"They found their place and filled it; they were able to find strength from one another despite great differences because they both were servants of Jesus Christ."

Speaking of this same pastoral relationship, Pastor

Roger L. Abington said: "Paul needs a Timothy; Timothy needs a Paul."* He went on to say: "All of us work in an environment of relationships. The relationship is what takes place between two or more persons. The quality of a relationship depends on the understanding each person has of himself and what he is to do and be in the relationship. I know of one church that had ten pastors over a period of twenty years. Each of these pastors had a rather difficult and unrewarding tenure. During each pastor's service, conflict between the pastor and deacons retarded the ministry of the church. It is clear that these pastors and deacons misunderstood their roles.

"Pastors and deacons are in a unique position to demonstrate to the church and community an ideal relationship. Flowing through them is the healing and redemptive power of God.

"Pastors and deacons must adopt a team concept. 'For we are partners working together for God' (1 Cor. 3:9, TEV).[1] Our work for God can be accomplished when we share together with God. We cannot do God's work single-handed.

"A team relationship between pastor and deacons develops when it is recognized that in Christ's church there are no 'solo performers.' The need for temperamental pastors and temperamental deacons to do their work solo is out of step with the team concept. Like the hand that needs the fingers to be the hand, we as pastors and deacons need one another to be a team.

---

[1] From the *Today's English Version* of the New Testament. Copyright © American Bible Society 1966, 1971. All succeeding quotations from this version are indicated by the abbreviation TEV in parenthesis.

The forward motion of the church in accomplishing the purposes of Christ is slowed or stopped when the pastor and deacons are not a team. It takes teamwork to accomplish the ultimate will of God."

Yes, now that you're a deacon, you have become a laborer together with your pastor in Christ's work. How do you and your pastor serve together? What similarities do you and your pastor share?

Pastor and Deacons Share Similar Qualifications

The qualifications for pastor and deacons are not set by man. God gave divine insight to Paul as he set forth qualities of spiritual life that both pastors and deacons are to possess. There is always grave danger lurking nearby when a church lowers the qualifications for either of these Christian leaders. God realized the need for these men to be stalwarts in Christian faith and practice by establishing such high standards.

Note the similarity of the spiritual qualifications that are established for the pastor and for the deacon in 1 Timothy 3. These qualifications speak of the kind of person that both leaders are "to be." They are to be spiritual men on a spiritual mission. The Scriptures do not speak of the exact work that either pastor or deacons are to do. Rather, God emphasized what these co-leaders in ministry are *to be*. Each should always be in the process of *becoming*. Someone has said that the greatest force in all the world is the power to become.

The Williams translation of 1 Timothy 3:1-13 states:

This is a saying to be trusted: "Whoever aspires to the office of pastor desires an excellent work." So the pastor must be a man above reproach, must have only one wife, must be temperate, sensible, well-behaved, hospitable, skillful in teaching; not addicted to strong drink, not pugnacious, gentle and not contentious, not avaricious, managing his own house well, with perfect seriousness keeping his children under control (if a man does not know how to manage his own house, how can he take care of the church of God?). He must not be a new convert, or else becoming conceited he may incur the doom the devil meant. He must also have a good reputation with outsiders, or else he may incur reproach and fall into the devil's trap.

Deacons, too, must be serious, sincere in their talk, not addicted to strong drink or dishonest gain, but they must continue to hold the open secret of faith with a clear conscience. They, too, should first be tested till approved, and then, if they are found above reproach, they should serve as deacons. The deaconesses [deacons' wives] too must be serious, not gossips; they must be temperate and perfectly trustworthy. A deacon too must have only one wife, and manage his children and household well. For those who render good service win a good standing for themselves in their faith in Christ Jesus.

Pastor and Deacons Share Ordination

When "the seven" were chosen by the early Jerusalem church, the church ordained them. In ordaining "the seven" an ancient Hebrew tradition of laying on of hands was followed by the church members. This was a beautiful ceremony and continues with us today in our Christian tradition of a service of ordination.

Pastors and deacons today share an ordination experience. Ordination does not give either pastor or deacons special authority or power. The ceremony simply demonstrates Christian love, affirmation, and fellowship. It says to both, "You have demonstrated to us your Christian maturity and devotion to Christ." To the pastor the ceremony says, "We affirm your expression that God has called you to proclaim, care, and lead the people of God as a Christian minister." To the deacon, the people say through the ordination services, "We have chosen you because we feel that God is alive in your life, and we want to follow you as our exemplar leader as you minister among us." Ordination does set one apart. The setting apart, however, is to service rather than to some special place of authority and power.

Pastor and Deacons Share a Similar Mission

Both pastor and deacons share a similar purpose and direction in life. Each serves Christ as a proclaimer of the gospel, a caring and compassionate minister, and a builder of Christian fellowship. Both serve to help God's work increase through his church. Energies are dedicated to building up the Body of Christ. Pastors and deacons depend on each other and the power of the Holy Spirit as they move together toward God's dynamic spiritual purpose.

Deacons and pastors share a similar work. The pastor is able often to give his full time to ministering to the flock. Deacons in most cases must give time to their daily job, but both serve the Lord gladly in a spiritual ministry.

There is a difference in pastor and deacon leadership roles. A church calls a pastor to be a generalist leader. In his leadership role, the pastor serves somewhat as a player-coach—an enabler. He is a grower of people. As a generalist leader the pastor leads the church to determine its spiritual mission. A pastor succeeds as a leader when he guides the church toward the attainment of its priority goals. The pastor, as a generalist leader, serves as chairman of the church council—the planning team that usually plans the total church program for church approval.

Deacons, on the other hand, are exemplar leaders. They serve as examples or models for fellow Christians to follow. Rather than providing general directional leadership as does the pastor, they serve as personal Christian examples to others. As exemplar leaders, deacons often serve behind the scene, out of the spotlight or central focus of activities. Deacon leadership is in harmony with the idea stated by an ancient Chinese philosopher: "A leader is best when people barely know that he exists; not so good when people obey and acclaim him; worse when they despise him. Fail to honor people, they fail to honor you; but a good leader, who talks little, when his work is finished they will say, we did this ourselves."

Pastor and Deacons Are Team Members

As I look back over my years of deacon service, some of my most fulfilling moments have come in fellowship with my pastor. He has enriched my soul and ministered to me in times of crisis and despair. You and your pastor, likewise, are partners in Christian service and fellowship. In the years ahead, you will look back and recall those experiences that you and your pastor have shared.

How can you and your pastor work more closely together? Here are some suggestions.

1. Understand your pastor and his work.

Have you ever thought what it would be like to be a pastor? Did you ever place yourself in his shoes and try to experience what he feels as he goes about his work each day? A key to partnership is this kind of empathy—understanding what your partner feels and experiences.

Pastor Ray O. Jones stated his feelings well as he wrote of a conversation he had with a nine-year-old boy.° The youngster had asked him, "What's it like to be a preacher?"

Pastor Jones replied: "Being a pastor is something like many other tasks in life, and yet it is unlike anything else in all the world. It's being loved and unloved, wanted and unwanted, understood and misunderstood. It's joy and sadness. It's heaven—and just to be honest—a bit of hell at times.

"My job keeps me in touch with birth and death, love and hate. As a pastor, I must be able to go from death to birth in a moment's notice. It's like talking with a drunken bum one minute and counseling with a beauty queen the next. It's climbing the stairs of a hospital wondering how many times I've climbed them before and how much—or how little—I've helped someone in pain.

"It's someone saying, 'If it hadn't been for you.' It's walking across a lonely graveyard after a funeral and wondering about the old man you buried. It's picking a man up out of the gutter when no one seems to care and telling him God cares, that God loves him and sent Christ into the world to die for his sins.

"There is no joy comparable to that of being a pastor. The heartaches and sorrows at times overwhelm us as shepherds of God's people, but the joy of serving, loving, and sharing with the people of God more than compensate for the hard and difficult hours."

Your pastor is a man just like you. He feels pain. Frustration sometimes comes his way. He has great hopes and dreams—some of which are not realized. And he needs a friend at times. He needs someone who will keep his confidences and share with him in moments of loneliness. He needs someone to share mutual dreams with and someone who will help him as a partner in pilgrimage. Your life will be enriched by becoming a friend of your pastor and a colleague and co-laborer with him.

2. Pray with and for your pastor.

Lift up your pastor in your daily prayers. Remember him while he is away. Ask that he experience spiritual power in his life and preaching. As you go about your daily work, breathe a silent prayer of thanksgiving for him and his ministry. Tell him occasionally how much he means to you.

Pastor Wayne Price once told how deacons had provided an undergirding support for him.° He had been leading some hospital visitation training sessions with his deacons. Soon afterwards he was taken to the hospital for emergency surgery. During his recuperation all of the deacons visited him at one time or another, but he remembered especially the visit of three of them.

"They didn't stay long," he said, "but they had obviously planned their visit. They told me that the deacons would arrange for daily visits to those church members who were in the hospitals. They told me of their plans to increase their visits to homebound church members. They promised to stay in close contact with me to help in worship planning and administration.

"Finally, one of the three deacons hesitated a bit, then spoke for the three of them. 'Brother Wayne,' he asked, 'May we say a prayer for you?' Then he prayed a beautiful prayer for my recovery. After this the deacons excused themselves, and they left with a promise to return the next evening.

"Their visit stirred me deeply. As a pastor, I had never thought that these men would be ministering to me someday as a hospital patient. The traditional roles were reversed. The pastor was being served by the deacon. I, the teacher, was being taught something about the role of brother and servant."

Pastors and deacons who work together do not find themselves in a fighting stance that sometimes disrupts a fellowship. John J. Hurt, editor of the Texas Baptist Standard, once told me of an incident that a pastor shared with him. The deacon said: "The pastor was new to the church, but already some differences of opinion had arisen regarding one of his recommendations. None of us wanted to turn down any such recommendation from the pastor—but at the time, none of us believed that we could support the recommendation.

"Joe was drafted to present our concerns to the

pastor. Then we had the experience of learning just what happened.

"It developed that Joe's first words were to the point: 'Pastor, some trouble is developing in the church, and I have been appointed to tell you about it.'

"The pastor was both surprised and troubled. 'Joe,' he said, 'let's kneel and pray about it first.'

"It took quite a bit of prodding to get more out of Joe, our emissary. It seems he won his freedom from the pastor's study by assuring the pastor only that 'we can handle it.'

"Joe's response was presented in brief summary for those who might think he failed the assignment. 'You can't get off your knees and start slugging with the pastor.'

"Yes, Joe was right. A reverent attitude in prayer often, as in this case, will solve most problems that develop between pastor and deacons."

The bonds of love and appreciation between pastor and deacons were made real to me when Pastor Dennis Hockaday told of the time when he lay desperately ill in the hospital. "A deacon came to the hospital door and quietly said to my wife, 'I knew that I could not go into the room. But I felt that at least I could come to the door, getting as close as possible to my pastor, and pray for him.' "

To alter a well-known motto, "The pastor and deacons who pray together—stay together."

A pastor once shared with me his love and admiration for a deacon in one of the early churches that he served.

"Deacon Anderson weighed about one hundred

pounds, but he was a giant in simple natural faith and love for his God.

"One Wednesday he came to the pastor's office and said: 'Circumstances prevent my coming to our prayer meeting tonight. I have had so many special new blessings from God I thought I would like to come by and ask you to share in my blessings, and that we should have a prayer meeting together.' I was delighted. He enumerated the blessings that were overwhelming his soul, then he knelt down to pray.

"Almost in the beginning of his prayer, he was overcome by his emotions and was unable to go on. After quite a bit of silence, he tried again. Again he choked with sobs. At last, with a voice of determination, he said, 'Lord, excuse me, I did not come before you to weep, but to praise you.' Then followed his wonderful prayer of praise and love. He grasped my hand and went out."

My pastor friend also told me of other times that Deacon Anderson bathed his soul with spiritual power. They prayed together often. "Deacon Anderson's praying was beautiful in natural childlike faith," my pastor friend said. "When he prayed, it was as a child talking to his father. He prayed with his eyes wide open. He seemed to be looking directly into his heavenly Father's eyes. His voice was in the natural conversation tone of a child's address to his father. Stilted and much worn pious phrases were absent. There was no evidence of rigid form in his prayers. I give an example. One occasion, he was leading the prayer and thanking God for the wonderful services of the preceding Sunday.

He said, 'Lord, we praise you for. . . .' He paused, turned about and said to our office secretary, 'Sister Brown, how many were in Sunday School yesterday?' She quietly answered, 'Five hundred and seventy-six.' Deacon Anderson then continued his prayer, 'Yes, Lord, we thank you for the five hundred seventy-six people in Sunday School yesterday.' "

3. Affirm your pastor.

Let your motto be, "Let me say a good word for my pastor." You will be affirmed as you affirm and support your pastor. Your life will be deepened and blessed as you say a good word to and for your pastor.

Over and over again pastors and deacons have related to me incidents where they have been strengthened through mutual partnership.

Pastor Conrad R. Willard told me once of the encouragement that a deacon gave to him in his first pastorate—a small country church. "When I began my ministry there I had preached only a few times. To say the least, I was inexperienced. Though from a sincere heart, some of those early sermons were hardly more than short talks on subjects related to religion.

"On occasions, too frequent I fear, both the idea and the delivery of that idea fell far short of what a sermon should be and do. The humble and helpful congregation could honestly say, 'He sure is sincere.' That was about all they could say for my early efforts at preaching. I remember those days when I had obviously been at my poorest, one good deacon would come up to me with a warm smile and friendly handshake. 'Brother Willard,' he would say, 'your sermon shore helped me a lot today.' Then as his hand met mine I would feel a bill tightly folded in his palm, so that no one would know he was paying me a little extra that day.

"I suppose both of us knew he was trying to lift my spirits and encourage me at a time of doubt and fear of failure. But neither ever mentioned it. He just gave me a little extra money, a word of encouragement, and a handclasp that told me he was a friend—my friend.

"Other pastors have told me he did the same for them when they began their ministry in that church. Only in heaven will we know the value of his service to God's kingdom through this simple, thoughtful act. His words were few, the amount of money small, but they always came at the moment they were needed most."

Pastor H. Cowen Ellis has served in the same church for many years. Years ago he related the following incident.

"Once one of the leading men in my church called me and asked more or less facetiously if I objected to his having a 'secret' meeting with a few of the members of our church. Knowing this man as I did and his character and intentions, I said to him that I had no reservations about any meeting he might lead. Two days later he came to my office with a letter. It was written in classic style and it was signed by twelve men. As I read the list of names, I knew the content of the letter was of the highest order, for these were twelve of the strongest men in my church. They were strong spiritually, intellectually, financially, and especially strong in leadership. In essence, the letter stated that these men were committing themselves to pray for me and for my ministry every day and to put themselves completely at my disposal to do anything I asked them to do any time day or night. They pledged themselves to give priority to any request I might make over any routine business activity, or responsibility, or social interest which they might have at the time."

Develop the habit of affirming your pastor—your partner in ministry.

Deacons would be a logical group to say, "Pastor, we love you" by sponsoring a Pastor Appreciation Day. This activity can be a meaningful experience in the life of a church. When people express their appreciation for their pastor, he, in turn, is strengthened and empowered to go on in his ministry for Christ in their midst. (See "List of Resources" for more information.)

4. Support your pastor.

Do you remember *Barrack Room Ballads* by Rudyard Kipling? In one of the ballads Kipling had one old soldier say,

> It ain't the individual nor the army as a whole,
> But the everlastin' teamwork of every bloomin' soul.

How close this ballad is to Paul's comment when he wrote, "For we are partners working together for God, and you are God's field" (1 Cor. 3:9, TEV).

A state Baptist paper once carried an article that portrays the heritage of a loyal deacon who supported his pastor. The article was written by a pastor who told of a service that was held for an elderly deacon of the church. "He is a living example of the ideal deacon," the pastor wrote. "When the first boards were nailed to our church, he was there. His ability to quote and use the Bible was exceeded only by his prayer life and practicing faith. Although he is not a young man any more, he is not opposed to new methods and young ideas if he believes them best for the church. Where others might have stood on sentiment, he has stood on faith. Never has he insisted on doing things, 'like we used to do' merely for the sake of old memories. He always considers what the Lord would have us do at this time for these people today."

At another recognition service I heard a pastor say of an eighty-one-year-old deacon, "He has been my spiritual support through all these years." When a special printed citation was presented to the honored deacon, he asked to say a word. "As a young man I established the policy of never criticizing my pastor nor my church. I have worked with fifteen pastors, and all of them are my friends. I commend this policy to the younger members of our church. This practice has brought me much happiness."

H. I. Hester, faithful pastor, teacher, and denominational leader, once told me of an incident that occurred in the 1930's while he was serving a church in Missouri. "One night a gang robbed our local bank. When the night watchman, who was a member of our church, appeared, he was shot down. He was rushed to the hospital but died four days later. This naturally created a sensation so that there was an overflow crowd at the funeral service. In this funeral service I spoke out strongly against such criminal acts. At the time the criminals had not been apprehended. Several years later I learned that three deacons at the service, fearing that some member of the gang might attack me on my way home, quietly followed my car the entire ten miles back to my home in Liberty, Missouri. This deed of courage and loyalty has meant much to me through the years."

5. *Enjoy fellowship with your pastor.*

Learn to respect each other's gifts. Rejoice that your partnership means he can depend on you and you can depend on him. Seek to learn from each other. Practice being open, honest, and loving in all your relationships. Risk revealing your real self to your pastor and allow him to share with you, always assured of your confidence.

Pastor Fred R. Skaggs tells of a deacon he calls "Mr. Harry." Mr. Harry had the gift of peacemaking. "He is a personification of what I think our Lord meant when he said, 'Blessed are the peacemakers' (Matt. 5:9). Like all churches, our church has had its share of problems and disagreements over the years. Although Mr. Harry rarely speaks his feelings during a business meeting, his presence always seems to say: 'Be careful! There are few things more important than our church's fellowship.' If Mr. Harry has food on his table, he will share it. If there is an opportunity for sharing the gospel story, he will take advantage of it. If he has money in his pocket and he knows someone has a real need for it, he will share that, too."

Pastor David R. Grant told me once about a deacon who had the gift of encouragement. "I was a student pastor and was baptizing only my second time. The baptism was to take place in a creek out in the open country, and I was frightened. There were only a few candidates to be baptized. But when I raised my hand to give the Scripture, my mind went blank. I stammered. I paused. My tongue was wrapped around my teeth and just about everything else went wrong. I do not know what I said, but I was terribly embarrassed. One of the outstanding deacons recognized my embarrassment. Immediately after the service was over, he took me to his pick-up truck and drove me down the road and started talking to me. He explained to me that if I never did anything any worse than that I would be all right as a pastor.

"Those words of encouragement have meant so much to me through the years. That same deacon recognized my need when I was asked to conduct my first funeral. I was contacted during Sunday School on the Sunday morning I was to conduct that funeral at two o'clock. Needless to say, I was again frightened beyond wits. The same deacon got me in the same pick-up truck and drove me down the same road and talked with me about what to say and how to say it. He was my teacher. He was a deacon with the gift of encouragement."

During World War II, I remember a Navy captain talking to a group of apprentice seamen at a training station. He spoke movingly about enjoying the experience of Navy life. His comments could well apply to enjoying the unique relationship of pastor and deacon. He said: "The sea demands more of men, but it gives more. No one who knows the meaning of the word 'shipmate' can fail to understand what it is that the sea gives, that the land can never give—the feeling of standing and working together, of individual strength and energy being pooled together for the safety and welfare of all, the sense of one's only antagonist being the elements that surround him."

Pastor and seminary teacher J. Winston Pearce, in *The Light on the Lord's Face*, tells this story: "On the bottom of a swimming pool at Monmouth, Illinois, at the center of the YMCA triangle was the reference to a Bible verse. It was John 17:21. A boy observed the reference but was unable to make out the wording. He dived and swam to the bottom over and over again. When the boy came up, he said to the coach, 'It says John 17:21, but what does that mean?' His coach answered, 'It says "that they may all be one." ' The boy's response was more perceptive than he knew, 'You sure have to go through a lot to find that out.' The coach responded, 'Yes, Son, we do. But it is worth the effort.' "

Pastor and deacons are partners in ministry. The benefits are many. You as a deacon will be strengthened. You will find out what it is to be a member of a team. Your spiritual life will be enriched. You will have opportunities to help others grow in Christ.

3
Translate Qualifications into Service

God gave you special gifts. How will you use your God-given gifts in deacon service?

I remember reading a poem by an unknown author entitled "White Elephants."

> I have an old box filled with things
> Like bolts and staples, nails and rings;
> And though I'm careful not to lose them
> I'm doubtful if I'll ever use them!

It is tragic for someone to go through life without ever realizing that God bestows to each person different and unique gifts. Did you ever stop to consider that you are a valuable "limited edition." You are unlike others about you. You are created like a snowflake or a fingerprint—distinctive! There is no one else just like you. You have been given special talents. God wants you to be fulfilled through use of these gifts in service to others in Christ's name.

Now that you are a deacon, give thought to your special gifts—or talents. What gifts do you bring for service as a deacon?

What kind of different gifts are there? Gifts are legion. Have you ever tried to list the gifts that God gave you? Do you have special talent for teaching, building fellowship, shepherding or caring, witnessing, reconciliation, stewardship, administration, prayer, speaking, or preaching? This is just the beginning, for God gives many talents.

Determine to find out your strengths so that you can give them in service as a deacon. Carve away at those areas in your life that impede your work for the Lord. Lay aside every weight that burdens you so that you can run the good race and fight the good fight.

R. L. Middleton, Christian businessman and popular writer, once shared an experience that two summer conference leaders had as they browsed through a gift shop near Asheville, North Carolina. They were looking at some wood carvings on display. Picking up a carved hound dog, one of the men asked the shop owner, "How in the world does someone go about carving a wooden hound dog?" The store owner pointed toward the corner and said: "See for yourself. There is the mountain man who whittles these hound dogs." The two men went over to the mountaineer who was whittling away. "How do you whittle a hound dog?" one of them asked. "Well, first I take a piece of wood about this size. Then I take my pocket knife and whittle away all the extra wood that don't look like no hound dog."

There is a message here for you. Carve and whittle away those extra things that keep you from using your special gifts for God in his service. Like the athlete who finds that his well-toned muscles fail through disuse, so a person will discover that his special gifts will melt away if they're not used actively. Your special gifts were given to you to help build up the body of

Christ as you minister in Christ's name.

Now that you are a deacon, move quickly to translate your spiritual qualifications into actual deacon service. Look at the qualifications the Bible sets for deacons.

The Bible Sets High Spiritual Qualifications

Churches are often tempted to lower the spiritual qualifications at deacon election time. A church should never fall to this temptation. God in his divine wisdom set the qualifications high because the work of the deacon is spiritual in its nature and requires men who are mature Christians.

Charles F. Treadway, outstanding denominational deacon leader, has summarized the scriptural qualifications for deacons well. Treadway lists and interprets the qualifications in this way:

A man of honest [good] report (Acts 6:3)—a good reputation among those in the church as well as those outside the church.

Full of the Holy Spirit (Acts 6:3)—bigness of character, in spiritual outlook and personal dedication.

Full of wisdom (Acts 6:3)—an ability to discern right and wrong and to stand for his convictions.

Full of faith (Acts 6:5)—like Stephen's, a deacon's faith requires him to risk himself and his possessions.

Grave (1 Tim. 3:8)—possesses Christian purpose, who has great reverence for spiritual matters, and whose word carries weight.

Not double-tongued (1 Tim. 3:8)—dependable and honest in relating to all persons, publicly and privately.

Not given to much wine (1 Tim. 3:8)—temperate in living, steward of good influence, doing all to the glory of God.

Not greedy of filthy lucre (1 Tim. 3:8)—a right attitude toward material possessions, never exploiting others for his own gain.

A holder of the faith (1 Tim. 3:9)—gives strength to the church fellowship and possesses spiritual integrity beyond reproach.

Tested and proved (1 Tim. 3:10)—demonstrates his commitment to ministry before being elected to serve as a deacon.

Blameless (1 Tim. 3:10)—a person against whom no charge of wrongdoing can be brought with success.

Christian family life (1 Tim. 3:11-12)—a person whose family is well cared for, whose family relationships are healthy and growing.

Husband of one wife (1 Tim. 3:12)—a model of faithful devotion to one spouse, committed to the sanctity of the marriage bond.

Ruling their children and their own houses well (1 Tim. 3:12)— loved and respected by all family members, caring for them as Jesus cared for others.

Bold in faith (1 Tim. 3:13)—holds firmly to what he believes, taking every opportunity for ministry.

Develop Your Spiritual Gifts

God will give you insight into how to develop for him. I remember seeing giant redwood trees on the West Coast. These trees, old beyond my imagination, made a deep impression on me. I thought about the vast power that it must take to get water from deep in the ground to the branches high above. I discovered, however, that the pressure did not push from below. Instead, the life-giving water was drawn by capillary action through the microscopic tubes. Life was drawn from the top rather than being pushed from the bottom. So God can draw out your finest qualities for his service if you will submit to him.

St. Augustine once prayed, "O Lord, grant that I may do thy will as if it were my will; so that I mayst do my will as if it were thy will."

1. Discover your special gifts.

Ask God's help. Pray about the matter. Search the Scriptures. Examine your life. Ask friends who know you well. Make an active search to find those talents that God has given to you. Discover your total capacity that can be used for him. What are your talents—your gifts?

Did you ever stop to think that Columbus did not really know what he had discovered. He saw only the outer edge of islands in the Caribbean Sea. He did not see the beauties of America and her soaring mountains, dark forests, riverways, great plains, and other marks of beauty. It may well be that you have seen only a portion of the person that you are—and the person you can become. But it will take work.

I once heard E. Stanley Jones tell a story about George Washington Carver, the renowned Negro scientist. Someone had asked George Washington Carver about his early work in scientific discoveries. Carver replied: "I took a peanut and put it in my hand. I turned it around—over and over. And then I said, 'Mr. Creator, what's in that peanut?' The creator answered me and said, "You have brains, George. Go and find out for yourself.' "

Mr. Deacon, God has blessed you. Discover your unique abilities. Use these gifts in his service.

2. *Nurture your gifts.*

Put your gifts to work. Develop your potential. Ask God's help. Seek to become the deacon that God wants you to be.

Years ago I read a newspaper feature written by a man who told of his student days in New York City. He related how he used to visit the magnificent Cathedral of St. John the Divine. Once a guide called his attention to a series of niches around the cathedral chancel. In each niche was carved the figure of a man who had been chosen as the greatest of his century. The first century was represented by St. Paul. Columbus represented the fifteenth; Washington, the eighteenth. The nineteenth had been awarded to Lincoln. It was the last niche that really caught his attention. This block of unshaped stone had not yet been carved. Still in rough hewn form, it represented the greatest man of the twentieth century. That name was yet to be chosen—for that person could well be in the process of becoming.

J. Winston Pearce relates a story in his book *Paul and His Letters* that represents imprisoned possibilities. He tells of a lumberman who found a nest of bird's eggs in the trunk of a tree. The nest had been made in the tree close to the ground. After the eggs had been laid, the resin had started to drip on a hot day. It ran until the opening was closed. As the months and years came and went, the bark of the tree completely closed the opening and hid the nest with the eggs. But for the closing, the birds would have blessed the world with their beautiful plumage and wonderful songs—imprisoned possibilities.

Nurture your gifts, Mr. Deacon. Put down deep roots and grow strong for the Lord. Resolve to grow like the giant redwood whose contribution to man lives beyond one man's life.

3. *Stir up the gifts of others.*

"Be thou an example," said Paul to Timothy (1 Tim. 4:12). As a deacon you are an exemplar leader. In addition to finding and using your gifts for God, be a part of stirring up the gifts of others. Paul said, "Stir up the gift of God which is in thee by the putting on of my hands" (2 Tim. 1:6). Paul had a God-appointed gift for helping people to ignite their own possibilities.

John Hendrix, writer and editor, in an article in *The Deacon,* said: "Throughout the New Testament, 'to stir up another's gifts' meant to excite the energies of that person, to release his potential for love and good works, to help him realize the fruits of the Spirit in his life. In our depths we have unlimited abilities to help each other, to summon the latent and varied gifts of the Spirit, to call into being the essence of other persons, and to challenge the unlived possibilities of many of our friends."

As you go about your work as a deacon, speak a word of encouragement and affirmation. In your visit to homes and hospital rooms, you will encounter persons who think they cannot hold on any longer. Share yourself with these lonely, often hostile persons. Be open and honest with them. Be willing to listen with your ears and your heart. Volunteer to help them carry their load for a while. Say a good word for the Lord. Encourage each person to turn to Christ for salvation and nurture.

Use Your Gifts in Deacon Service

A pastor in Alabama told me of a deacon who had the glowing gift of affirmation. The pastor was in his study late on Sunday afternoon seeking to put the final touch to the evening message.

A knock sounded, and in walked the deacon, hesitatingly—almost shyly. "Pastor," he began, "forgive the interruption. But I just had to tell you something. Your message this morning was from Jacob's well. It thrilled my soul. God is using you here in our midst." He continued, "I'm praying that he will give you power like that again tonight." With that he slipped out. That night the pastor preached with a new strength.

T. B. Lackey, long-time pastor and state Baptist leader, once told me of an incident that occurred early in his ministry. "One Sunday my preaching was unusually poor. I was discouraged. I felt as if I should throw up my hands and quit. When the service ended, a deacon came and put his arm around me and said, 'Brother Bert, I believe in you.' That is all he said. That is all he needed to say. If he believed in me, I had to be a success. I have often wondered what would have happened if God had not blessed me with a deacon like that."

How will you use your gifts? Where will your place of service be? As you visit in homes or hospitals and as you encounter people in your daily business, you will be able to minister to them. Now that you are a deacon, dedicate yourself to being the kind of deacon God wants you to be. Here are some suggestions for service.

1. Serve as a caring person.
Each deacon needs to develop a caring spirit that causes him to stop, reach out, and help persons in need. Caring should become a continuing way of life rather

than an isolated action, turned on and off as an electric light.

A friend told me the story of a little girl who was sent to the store by her mother. When the child returned late, the mother said, "Why did it take you so long?"

The little girl replied, "I saw Annie, and she had dropped her doll and broken it."

The mother asked, "Did you help her fix it?"

"No, Mother, but I sat down and helped her cry."

How many times in your life have you ever needed a friend who was willing to sit down and help you cry? Such a caring concern is the ministry of today's deacon. Caring is being willing to make yourself vulnerable.

Ralph Atkinson, seminary educator, wrote in *Church Administration:* [1] "If most physicians prescribed medicine the way some church members minister, few sick people would ever recover. Unlike the doctor who prescribes continued dosage of the healing drugs for his patient, most church members minister as if they believe in one shot, magic cures for problems of the needy. A basket of groceries at Christmas, a tiny ejection of cash in a crisis, or a bundle of worn-out clothes—and we hope the misery of a face will vanish. Real help demands prolonged, sustained, involvement. It means that each church member will help fewer people, but help them significantly. It requires patience, trust, acceptance, and most of all, love."

---

[1] *Church Administration* is a magazine published quarterly by The Sunday School Board of the Southern Baptist Convention.

2. Serve as a Christian witness.

I agree with the speaker who said that Christianity must be as contagious as the measles.

Such a spiritual contagion was found in the lives of Stephen and Philip—two of the original "seven." It is easy to see why these two men were chosen by their fellow Christians to minister through the Jerusalem church.

The Deacon Tapes (see "List of Resources") had this to say about Stephen: "Significantly every time his name was called, his personal spiritual qualifications were described. Stephen was obviously a man of great faith. His life demonstrated a personal experience with the Lord. His life was filled with the Holy Spirit. Stephen must have been a winsome individual. Even his enemies saw that Christian quality of life that made him different. His great personal concern for people was seen in his preaching. Yes, preaching as a layman. Even when he knew his Christian message would bring his death, he spoke out lovingly and forcefully of Christ. He had a concern for the spiritual welfare of his enemy. Probably knowing that he would soon be murdered, he had to share the gospel with others. As Stephen lay dying, crushed by the stones hurled at him, he prayed, 'Lord, let not this sin be laid to their charge.' Here was a man whose concern with the spiritual needs of people was so great that his dying breath was a prayer for them."

3. Serve as an exemplar leader.

Deacons are chosen by their fellow church members

because the members see in them qualities of spiritual maturity. Both Christians and non-Christians observe the daily lives of deacons. As Christian examples, deacons serve as exemplar leaders to others. Paul admonished Timothy to "be an example of the believer" (1 Tim. 4:12).

Ernest E. Mosley says in *Called to Joy:* "Deacons are in a prime position to serve as exemplar leaders and help the church accomplish its mission. They are selected leaders in the church. As they support the organizational life of the church, they set an example for others. They lead others to participate through their model of service. Whenever there is enthusiastic participation by deacons in a church organization, there will likely be enthusiasm and vitality in the organization. Such leadership is valuable to a church."

Walter A. Bennett, Jr., pastor and denominational leader, said:* "One of the greatest opportunities for leadership by the deacon is through his exemplary service—his leadership by example. Once a person is elected a deacon, he no longer has a choice as to whether he will set an example. The only decision concerns the kind of example he will be.

"Church activities are much more successful when deacons give them verbal endorsement and active participation. One deacon with an indifferent attitude toward a revival or visitation campaign can weaken the effectiveness of his entire group. Deacons can support their church's program of work by: (1) accepting church responsibilities wherever their talent may be used, (2) attending faithfully the regular meetings of the church, (3) promoting and interpreting the work of the church to members, new members, and other persons, and (4) encouraging and appreciating the service of others in the church."

What kind of Christian example will you be as a deacon?

4. Serve as a builder of Christian fellowship.

How can the deacon contribute to the building of Christian fellowship in his church?

A favorite New Testament passage of mine is Luke 24. It tells of two of Jesus' followers walking the lonely, dusty road to the little village of Emmaus. They were dejected, confused, lonely. Gloom and defeat covered them as did the dust of the winding road. The reason for their depression—the Master had been crucified and buried. They had just received word that now his body was missing from the tomb—possibly stolen by graverobbers.

As they walked and talked, a stranger joined them and began to tell of God's divine plan for sending a Messiah.

The stranger, accepting their invitation, stopped with them to eat supper. "And it came to pass, as he sat at meat with them, he took bread, and blessed it, and brake it, and gave to them. And their eyes were opened, and they knew him" (Luke 24:30-31).

Then comes my favorite passage: "And they said one to another, Did not our hearts burn within us, while he talked with us by the way, and while he opened to us the scriptures?" (Luke 24:32).

What a description of Christian fellowship—"Did not our hearts burn within us."

Are there some lessons here that will aid deacons to help the church build a healthy, vibrant fellowship?

Verses 14-15—"And they talked together of all these things which had happened. And it came to pass, that, while they communed together and reasoned, Jesus himself drew near, and went with them."

When Christians meet together—talk of Christ, have two-way communication with each other regarding Christ's work in their lives—there is usually fellowship. When Christians are spiritually walking down the same road together, there is usually fellowship.

Aren't Christians promised "where two or three are gathered together there I will be." Deacons can help enrich fellowship by helping the church members to gather regularly for worship of God. It is when Christians fail to walk and talk together in Christ that fellowship cools. Fellowship is a by-product of expectant, joyful worship.

As a deacon, you can enhance the spirit of worship by assisting in worship activities such as the observance of the Lord's Supper and baptism, ushering, public prayer, and Scripture reading.

Your personal spirit as you participate in church business can build the warm atmosphere of fellowship. Your presence shows your interest in the total welfare of your church. Ability to share a viewpoint yet realize that others have their opinions also builds fellowship. Demonstration that you desire to do the will of the Holy Spirit is a witness for fellowship. Joining in with the majority after a decision has been made, even though you voted differently, builds fellowship.

Bruce H. Price, pastor and author, once told me of a deacon whose actions demonstrate an abiding concern for building Christian fellowship. "A deacon in a former pastorate was on a special committee to recommend to the church whether we should enter a building program at once or not to build.

"This deacon, who was a wealthy man, successful in business, dedicated to the Lord, and active in all the life of the church, opposed the building plans in committee meeting, saying we were not financially able to build—and the building plans should be delayed for several years. He was very determined to carry his point.

"However, after much discussion the committee voted to recommend to build at once. This deacon voted no. Two of his close friends did not vote. Four other committee members voted in favor of building immediately.

"As soon as the vote was announced, the deacon arose and said, 'Let me see the plans again.' He expressed his pleasure with the plans and was a public supporter of the undertaking. He was one of the largest financial contributors to the new building. From the moment of the vote he was completely devoted to the project."

Here was a deacon who believed in maintaining a warm, Christian fellowship where church members could say, "Did not our hearts burn within us."

4
Sharpen Your Skills
for Deacon Service

Now that you are a deacon, you have great work to do! Just as a young military recruit must learn new skills in order to serve effectively, so you must train for deacon service. There is both thrill and skill involved in serving as a deacon.

A friend told me of two businessmen who were on their way home from work. Their route took them past the practice field of a local high school. A crowd had gathered along the sidelines to watch the practice scrimmage. The first game was still three weeks away. The two men parked their car by the curb to watch. Calling out to one of the students nearby, one of the businessmen said, "Hey, what's going on?"

With a wide grin, the youngster answered, "They are *canning touchdowns* for the team to use in September."

What an illustration! The young boy had spoken wisdom far beyond his years. Games are not always won in September and October. Much of the victory results from hard work done under the summer sun of August as the team trains for the upcoming season.

Educators report that the average person uses approximately 10 percent of his potential. Only about

10 percent! This means that there is a total of 90 percent of potential that goes untapped. This is like a mighty river crashing over the brink of a waterfall— unused, unharnessed, unproductive.

You need not let your potential go unharnessed. Remember the verse you learned years ago: "Study to show thyself proved unto God a workman that needed not to be ashamed." You can grow! But you must study and train for new responsibilities.

Around the nation, adult education is booming. Adults are going back to school. Businessmen are learning that training is a lifelong activity. You can and should equip yourself to serve as a deacon. Your training will provide you new skills. You will be energized just as a battery is recharged through steady use.

Remember how Jesus gave priority to training his disciples. He knew that these followers would live on long after he had returned to the Father. Jesus took his small band of unskilled individuals and taught them. They developed into a team that had a will to win. They went on and did their part in setting their world aflame for Christ. There is so much to be done. But new skills are needed if you are to serve effectively. You can become the most effective deacon you want to be. The power to become is at your disposal.

Ken Chafin says in his refreshing book *Help, I'm a Layman* that a climate must be created for growth. He lists these elements that must be present if the climate of growth is to be established.[1]

"Be honest about your need for future development.

---

[1] (Waco, Texas: Word Books, 1966).

"Keep an openness to new truth.

"Involve yourself with other Christians in worship, Bible study, and fellowship.

"Maintain a friendship with non-Christians so that your life can influence theirs.

"Accept responsibility in your church.

"Make an effort to share your faith with others."

Ask yourself, Am I willing to learn the new skills required of a deacon today? Will I really give the time to developing new growth lines in my life? Am I as committed to my deacon ministry as the high school football team was committed to "canning touchdowns" for the coming season? If so, diligent work is required to make ready.

A favorite football coach of mine, who is known for his winning teams, is reported to have this sign in his office. "The harder I work, the luckier I get." Will you commit yourself to the disciplined life of one in training?

Teddy Roosevelt used to say, "The man that thinks he has arrived is already on the return trip." The growing deacon is willing to study—train—retool. His growth is alive and real. He is unlike the modern plastic flower that only looks alive.

I still recall my dismay when I first visited a "mothball fleet" following World War II. Scores of giant Navy vessels lay rusting at anchor. A minimum of effort had been made to preserve the ships by spraying vital parts with plastic coverings—thus the name "mothball fleet." As a sailor, I had known first-hand the beauty of sleek Navy ships alert and battle ready. I could not believe my eyes when I saw those rusting ships that once were manned by crews possessed with purpose and vision. What a change! Now the ships rode silently at anchor. Rust ate away at them hungrily. They were chained together as galley slaves. Their only movement was the creaking groans of vessels at anchor.

Now that you are a deacon you cannot rest at anchor—uninvolved—untrained. The battle needs you! You need the battle!

There are excellent deacon training resources available for you to use in sharpening your skills for service. See the section "List of Resources."

Strengthen Your Personal Spiritual Development

Your fellow church members have seen in you qualities of Christian maturity. You obviously have served well and are trusted by your Christian friends. As you look at your own life, you probably see areas that need strengthening. This is only natural—and a good sign. God has given you a big job to perform for him. Your opponent is devastating. But the Holy Spirit will empower you if you seek his help.

What about your prayer life? Do you spend time daily with the Lord? The Holy Spirit wants to be your comfort and guide. You have the promise of his presence. Has prayer become a live, viable, enriching experience for you?

Are you reading the Bible regularly? Do you have a systematic plan for studying the Scriptures and letting them speak to you? It is difficult to find a block of time for regular devotional reading and intense Bible study. Do you take a Bible with you as you travel? Have you learned to turn to the Gideon Bible in the motel room at the end of a busy work day? The Scriptures will provide you strength and nourishment.

Develop Skills for Improving Interpersonal Relations

In one sense, every person is a human chemist. You work in a laboratory of interpersonal relationships. The make-up of persons about you differs greatly. In a chemical laboratory a chemist knows intimately the characteristics of the chemical elements and compounds with which he works. He has respect for the properties of each chemical. He knows how different chemicals react when mixed with others, and he respects these chemical reactions.

Now that you are a deacon, you need to learn the skills of being a human chemist. As a builder of church fellowship, you have a responsibility to know and accept people as they are. A chemist does not dislike a certain chemical because it behaves in an uncharacteristic manner. So you as a human chemist should not show surprise or hostility when individuals react emotionally. The forerunner of today's deacons, "the seven," came into being because there was a human chemistry problem. A difficulty in relationship developed. Guided by the Holy Spirit, these mature Christian men sought out the facts, dealt with them lovingly and objectively, and preserved harmony of fellowship.

Learn to respect and listen to the other side of the story. Keep in mind that people who hurt are often sensitive and fearful of revealing their true selves. Do not be judgmental. Listen attentively as tney share their frustration. People need someone who will lend a sympathetic ear. Don't be tempted to lose track of the conversation in an effort to think ahead to what you will say. One writer expressed it well when he said

> To other people's woes,
> I lend a sympathetic ear,
> However sad it is to hear,
> Their real or fancied throes.
> I pay to every gloomy line,
> attention undiminished
> Because I plan to start on mine
> the moment theirs are finished.[2]

Strengthen Your Competence in Personal Witnessing

Several years ago I hailed a cab in downtown Atlanta and asked the driver to take me to the airport. Sitting in the back seat, preoccupied with the events of the day, I suddenly realized that the driver was talking to me. As I listened, it became evident that he was witnessing to me—in a courteous and concerned manner. I said to him, "You are a Christian, aren't you?"

"Yes," he replied. "How did you know?" We rode along together and talked as two Christian brothers. In the course of the conversation, he asked me, "I bet you wonder why I am a cab driver?"

Before I could reply, he continued, "Me and my wife were talking about this just the other day." They had discussed the kind of work that he would do for the remainder of his life. "I make pretty good money

[2] John Drakeford, *The Awesome Power of the Listening Ear* (Waco: Word Books, 1967) p. 47.

as a cab driver, particularly for a man with so little education," he said. He and his wife, however, had made a decision that he would continue driving a cab. Why? "You don't know how many broken hearts sit on that back seat, Mister," he said. "Where could I find a job that allowed me to meet so many hurting people and let me tell them about my Savior."

About that time we passed a little Baptist church. Glowingly, he turned, and pointed it out to me. "That's my church!—I love those people, and they love me."

I have often thought of this man and the witness that he must be having in Atlanta. Here was a man who had found the excitement of putting his religion into daily life. He had learned the secret of happy, joyous witnessing. True, he did not know a great deal of theology. True, he was not skilled in the fine points of scriptural knowledge. But he had found the secret of effective witnessing. He could tell others what the Lord had done for him. He had also found purpose in his life. He had combined his job with his Christian experience.

Memorize some basic Scripture passages. Appropriate occasions will come when you can share some of the great promises of the Scriptures with someone who has lost all hope. Learn how to use your Bible. Keep a Bible or a pocket-size New Testament with you. Become comfortable in its use. Learn the books of the Bible so that you can easily find a passage when talking to someone.

Make the plan of salvation a part of you. Do not follow it slavishly, but know the basic steps in leading someone to Christ. As you study your Bible, develop the practice of underlining passages for emphasis. While in college I learned that it was far better to buy a secondhand textbook that had been used by a good student than to purchase a new book. In addition to saving money, the used book usually had the important sections already marked by the previous owner. The markings quickly called my attention to important content.

I have found it a good practice to memorize certain Scripture passages. These passages serve as an encouragement to me in times of disappointment or grief. You, too, will find many occasions to use the Scriptures appropriately as you minister. Long ago I listed some specific Scripture references on the inside cover of my Bible. You may find this practice helpful too. If so, you will need to do some study to determine which passages are appropriate for your use.

Here are some Bible passages that have been meaningful to me:

ALL HAVE SINNED
1. "For all have sinned, and come short of the glory of God"—Romans 3:23.
2. "If we say that we have no sin, we deceive ourselves, and the truth is not in us"—1 John 1:8.
3. "The heart is deceitful above all things, and desperately wicked"—Jeremiah 17:9.

LOST WITHOUT CHRIST
1. "He that believeth on him is not condemned: but he that believeth not is condemned already, because he hath not believed in the name of the only begotten Son of God"—John 3:18.
2. "The soul that sinneth, it shall die"—Ezekiel 18:20.
3. "There is none righteous, no, not one"—Romans 3:10.

God Loves Sinners

1. "God so loved the world, that he gave his only begotten Son, that whosoever believeth in him should not perish, but have everlasting life"—John 3:16.

2. "God commendeth his love toward us, in that, while we were yet sinners, Christ died for us"—Romans 5:8.

3. "Who shall separate us from the love of Christ?"—Romans 8:35.

Christ Will Save You Now

1. "Today if ye will hear his voice, harden not your hearts"—Hebrews 3:15.

2. "If we confess our sins, he is faithful and just to forgive us our sins, and to cleanse us from all unrighteousness"—1 John 1:9.

3. "Whosoever will, let him take the water of life freely"—Revelation 22:17.

4. "Verily, verily, I say unto you, He that believeth on me hath everlasting life"—John 6:47.

5. "Him that cometh to me I will in no wise cast out"—John 6:37.

Christ Will Keep You

1. "Yea, he shall be holden up: for God is able to make him stand"—Romans 14:4.

2. "Kept by the power of God through faith unto salvation ready to be revealed in the last time"—1 Peter 1:5.

3. "I give unto them eternal life; and they shall never perish, neither shall any man pluck them out of my hand"—John 10:28.

Proof of Your Salvation

1. "Therefore if any man be in Christ, he is a new creature: old things are passed away; behold, all things are become new"—2 Corinthians 5:17.

Develop as a Caring Person

W. L. Howse, distinguished seminary professor and denominational leader, once told me of a Sensitive Plant he had seen in South America. It was about the size of a tabletop. When you touched it at any point, the

entire plant shuddered visibly. As I have thought of
the responsiveness of this plant, I have wished that
I, too, could be as responsive in spirit. Now that you
are a deacon, you need to develop a responsive, empathetic, sensitive spirit. What a joy it is to be a caring
person—sensitive to needs about you.

C. W. Brister says in his book *People Who Care:*
"Do Christians have a right to avoid getting 'involved'
with people in trouble? Christ was always taking a
towel and girding himself in order to minister to others
and to set an example for believers. Just as he preached
'deliverance to the captives' in the days of his flesh,
he works through Christians in order to bring hope
to men today."

Brister goes on to say: "We must not be indifferent
when crises come. People are weak and need God's
help. The best way to learn what their real needs are
is by listening and responding to the facts and feelings
they express. Listening and responding to facts and
feelings of other people is not an inherited quality.
Sharing another's plight and pilgrimage is a learned
experience. Some people need a course in remedial
listening. Others should practice keeping confidences.
Do not expect someone to bare his soul and share secret
sins or hurts unless you intend to share something of
yourself. Your interest and comradely care will prove
more effective than giving advice or rejecting a wor-
rier."

As a caring deacon you will encounter situations that
will require you to have a foundation for understanding
the forces at work. A comprehension of what is taking

place will enable you to minister more effectively. You will also be able to serve with assurance and confidence if you are prepared for your ministry in homes, hospitals, or other places where you visit.

You will often encounter the universal emotion of grief as a deacon. Develop an understanding of grief. Sharpen your skills to help you minister lovingly to persons suffering the trauma of grief.

Read books for a better understanding. An excellent resource is *Facing Grief and Death* by William P. Tuck. Another is the book *Good Grief* by Granger E. Westbury. These books will provide skills to help you comfort those who hurt.

Paul reminds the Christian, "You may not grieve as others do who have no hope" (1 Thess. 4:13). The Christian will encounter grief, for grief is a natural human response. The Christian has a spiritual resource that he can call for support that is unknown to the non-Christian.

"A first step in ministering to the bereaved is a realization that many occasions other than death spark grief," says Robert D. Dale in his book *Growing a Loving Church.* "Everyone grieves. We grieve because we periodically feel loss. Death is the most obvious loss that triggers our grief. Think of times, other than death, when you have felt loss and, therefore, grief. Here's a list to jog your memory.

"When your child enrolled in school or college.

"When your son was inducted into military service.

"When your youngster got married.

"When you retire.

"When you suffered a financial reverse.

"When you got a different job or a new boss."

The book *Good Grief* gives insight into the various stages of grief. When one of your assigned family members suffers grief, you can be of far more help if you understand where the person is in the grief process. Most grieving persons pass through several stages. The rate of progress through which a person passes some or all these stages of grief differs with the individual.

You will observe a response such as uncontrollable crying or laughter. Some persons may experience a calm serenity that causes people to say, "Isn't she holding up well." In actuality, the person may be under the temporary anesthesia of *shock*.

There will be *expressed emotions* from the person in grief. "I just can't believe it happened" or "This can't be happening to me" will be spoken over and over.

Dark, black *depression and utter loneliness* will usually occur. The bright light of life's sun seems to fade from view. Don't be surprised to hear comments of doubt.

Even *physical illness*—real or imagined—will result. The person in grief may not want to eat or sleep.

Some persons experience a *sense of panic*. For the first time they may be encountering a situation without the resources adequate for the task. They dwell continually on the problem and are deeply troubled.

Sometimes an overpowering *feeling of guilt* will flood over the one in grief. Some sharp criticism or neglect is recalled. They say, "If I had been a better father" or "If I had known what she was going through." These are normal feelings of guilt and neurotic expressions of guilt. In your deacon training, seek help in understanding behavior characteristics so that you can refer persons in need to professionals for assistance.

Hostility and resentment is a stage of grief you can anticipate. Don't be overly disturbed if a person lashes out at you or someone else—even at God. Don't be shocked or angered at such conduct from a friend in grief.

Continual inability to function normally is another stage of grief. The person has extreme *difficulty returning to usual activities* of daily living.

Gradually hope returns and life begins to come back. The gloom begins to fade and the one in grief begins to *adjust to reality*.

You can be of genuine help to persons in grief in many ways. Your presence will show that you care. Do not be overly concerned about what you will say or do. Just being there is the first essential. Practice listening. Let your friend talk to you. Give your total attention.

Try to keep advice to a minimum. A grieving person needs to ventilate emotions. It takes hours of talking and sharing to clear away the overpowering grief.

Resist the temptation to say, "Don't cry," or, "Now you must hold up." Somehow we have assumed that people are not supposed to cry. If this were true, God would have not created tear ducts. Crying is a normal, healing act that helps wash away the grief that floods our being. It may be the shortest verse in the Bible, but it is one of the most comforting in time of trouble—"Jesus wept!" (John 11:35). And don't forget to follow through. Follow-through is just as essential to the grieving person as it is to your golf swing. It takes time and physical effort to work through the grief process. Keep going back after the initial visit. After the shock wears away is when you are really needed.

Your deacon ministry will take you to hospitals and home sick-rooms. You will be far more effective if you will develop a few skills in visitation—so that your visit will be a blessing to the patient rather than a bad experience.

Ask your deacon chairman to consider scheduling some training sessions during regular deacon meetings. Your pastor or a local hospital chaplain might lead these training sessions.

Consult your church librarian for books that will help you. There are excellent resources available that are both practical and easy to read. One of the best books I've read is *Don't Sit On the Bed* by William G. Justice. This handbook for visiting the sick is packed with help for the layman.

A brief look at some of the section headings demonstrate the author's practical approach:

- Always knock before entering a room
- Do not carry stirred emotions from room to room
- Show no shock at what you see
- Let the patient choose the course of the conversation
- Total silence is often appropriate

- Do not be insulted by your patient's words or attitudes
- Do not offer false optimism
- Do not try to out-diagnose the doctor
- Keep your troubles to yourself
- Respect other patients
- Make your visit brief

I have often used the small, attractive booklet *The Up Side of Down* in my visitation of the sick. It can be given or mailed to a patient. This booklet contains several pages of appropriate devotional thoughts as well as having space for listing such information as visitors, cards, flowers, etc.

Develop Skills for Building Fellowship

Building and maintaining Christian fellowship is a primary job for the deacon. Fellowship is built as a result of witnessing, caring, and exemplar leadership. Fellowship is a by-product that comes when Christian people gather and express honest affirmation of each other. Fellowship is a derivative of prayer, singing, and study of the Scriptures. Fellowship results when Christians feel the closeness and concern of one person for another. You can be instrumental in building Christian fellowship by your openness, honesty, and caring attitude. Building and maintaining fellowship has been a responsibility of the deacons since "the seven" were first appointed in the Jerusalem church.

A writer in *Proclaim*,[3] the journal of biblical preach-

---

[3] *Proclaim* is a magazine published quarterly by The Sunday School Board of the Southern Baptist Convention.

ing, told of a man visiting in Guatemala. As he travelled through the countryside he saw numerous fenceposts along the roadside that had become living trees. The writer said, "I inquired of one of the missionaries who was familiar with the situation and he told me that the warm, moist climate accounted for this unusual sight." He continued "If a post is alive when it is put in the ground, the climate here is such that it will grow."

Your work as a deacon is to help develop a climate of fellowship in your church that will enable persons to grow toward spiritual maturity.

Develop your skills in being a member of a group, such as a committee meeting, deacon meeting, or church business session. Learn to discern the dynamic of group discussion. Listen for what people are saying by their words and action. Listen for the real problems that may not yet be spoken. Acquire skill for interpreting the feelings of persons who may not be active in the discussion. Learn how tactfully to involve as many persons as possible into the discussion. Do not be fearful of differences of opinion, for a lasting solution is not usually found until all major issues are surfaced. Occasionally seek to summarize the major points of agreement or disagreement. Clarify. Ask for additional input. Learn to approach a problem objectively. Develop the skills of openness and honesty. Grow in your ability to hear what the other person is saying. When you are looking for the best solution, you must welcome ideas from every source.

You can use these skills in many ways as a deacon.

There will be occasions when you visit with church families that may have had their feelings hurt—either actually or imagined.

Your ministry is one of reconciliation. You are a peacemaker—a builder of Christian harmony. So live that you can say in words similar to those of Christ: "As my Father sent me into the world, so I send you into the world on a mission of reconciliation. Both speak and live the good news of God's reconciling love."

Opportunity will come in church business meetings for you to use your skills of reconciliation. Demonstrate how a person can participate actively in a discussion without feeling that he "lost" if the vote goes against his particular position on an issue.

In monthly meetings of the deacons, there will be times when sensitive issues will be confronted. Develop the skills and spirit of a peacemaker. You are the guardian of Christian fellowship.

Grow as an Exemplar Leader

Be willing to get involved. Your fellow Christians have affirmed you because they believe you have qualities of leadership. Let your eyes and voice express your joy for living. By personal example demonstrate to those about you that you are enriched by participation in your church program. Live a disciplined Christian life victoriously. Seek out difficult but fulfilling jobs to perform. It is said that Mrs. Eleanor Roosevelt always carried the following prayer in her purse: "Our Father, who has set a restlessness in our hearts and made us all seekers after that which we can never fully find

. . . keep us at tasks too hard for us, that we may be driven to Thee for strength."

I know a deacon whose personal life is an example in Christian witness. As a surgeon he is known for his medical skill. But he is known also for his personal devotion to Christ. A nurse said of him: "He is not a miracle worker even though he is the most skilled surgeon I have ever known. I have seen him pause during an operation and say, 'God, please guide my hands—for only you can save the life of the patient.' "

A mayor of a large city in the South serves as a Baptist deacon. His example for morality and honesty is known abroad. Christ is a vital part of his life. Even though he is involved in countless meetings with the leaders of his city, you can find him on Wednesday night at his church taking part in the prayer service. He told me once, "I travel widely in the course of my work, but I need the spiritual enrichment that comes from being in my place at church on Sunday morning and evening." We talked of his ambassadorial function as mayor and the daily temptation of social drinking at formal banquets and social gatherings. "My work requires me to represent the city at scores of meetings," he said. "But it didn't take long for the word to get around that the mayor doesn't drink." Here is a deacon whose Christian character speaks boldly as an exemplar leader.

5
Become a Caring Witness

Now that you are a deacon, share your Christian witness with those you meet daily. The heart of deacon work today centers around the ministry of being a caring witness. This chapter seeks to interpret how you "become" a caring witness.

Set "Becoming" as Your Goal

Your fellow church members have already seen in you qualities of spiritual maturity. Your selection, election, and ordination indicates that others have already been influenced by your Christian witness. But now the challenge is even greater—to continue to grow spiritually as you serve as a deacon.

There is an ancient truth that says, "You become what you think about." The person who thinks of worthy, wholesome, and purposeful goals becomes like his goals. In like manner, the man who sets his mind on the low and unworthy takes on those same characteristics himself.

Gardening has been a hobby of mine for years. Enriching the soil has become a continuing backyard project with me. Throughout the year, I feed the soil with compost and other organic materials. Gradually, my garden has changed from weak clay soil to rich black loam. Tomatoes, corn, or beans grow with profusion in this revitalized garden soil. But if I were to plant thistles or dandelions instead of vegetable seeds, they too would grow in profusion.

My garden soil doesn't care what seeds I plant. So it is with your mind, your heart, and your soul. "Whatsoever a man soweth, that shall he also reap." If you plant worthless seed during your deacon tenure, you will reap a worthless harvest. If you set your mind on becoming a productive deacon witness, you will grow toward becoming the deacon you want to be. Keep in mind that you have additional help beyond your own. Remember the Scripture passage, "Whatsoever ye ask in prayer, believing, that shall ye also receive."

How can you become a deacon who is a caring witness? What are some characteristics of a deacon that is growing in spiritual maturity and practice?

A "Becoming" Deacon Heeds Christ's "Go Ye"

A "becoming" deacon will follow the command Christ gave to his disciples. He said, "*Go ye* into all the world." This was not a mere suggestion or a tentative proposal. Christ stated "Go ye" as an imperative. Just as human muscles develop through steady exercise, so your spiritual life develops as you tell others of your Christian experience. When Andrew met the Master, he immediately went to get his brother Simon. James went to his brother John to tell him about the Master. Both Andrew and James were caring witnesses to their brothers, Simon and John.

Philip continued his pilgrimage of "becoming" after completing his initial work as part of "the seven." He had served well in helping to resolve the fellowship problem in the early Jerusalem church. But the Bible tells of his continuing witness. "Then Philip went down to the city of Samaria, and preached Christ unto them. And the people with one accord gave heed unto the things which Philip spake, hearing and seeing the miracles which he did" (Acts 8:5-6).

Today's deacon can learn much about spiritual growth (the process of becoming) by studying the account of Philip's witness. Acts 8:26-40 records:

And the angel of the Lord spake unto Philip, saying, Arise and go toward the south unto the way that goeth down from Jerusalem unto Gaza, which is desert. And he arose and went: and, behold, a man of Ethiopia, an eunuch of great authority under Candace, queen of the Ethiopians, who had the charge of all her treasure, and had come to Jerusalem for to worship, was returning, and sitting in his chariot reading Esaias the prophet. Then the Spirit said unto Philip, Go near and join thyself to this chariot. And Philip ran thither to him, and heard him read the prophet Esaias, and said, Understandest thou what thou readest? And he said, How can I, except some man should guide me? And he desired Philip that he would come up and sit with him. The place of the scripture which he read was this, He was led as a sheep to the slaughter; and like a lamb dumb before his shearer, so opened he not his mouth: . . . And the eunuch answered Philip, and said, I pray thee, of whom speaketh the prophet this? of himself, or of some other man? Then Philip opened his mouth, and began at the same scripture, and preached unto him Jesus. And as they went on their way, they came unto a certain water: and the eunuch said, See, here is water; what doth hinder me to be baptized? And Philip said, If thou believest with all thine heart, thou mayest. And he answered and said, I believe that Jesus Christ is the Son of God. And he commanded the chariot to stand still: and they went down both into the water, both Philip and the eunuch; and he baptized him. And when they were come up out of the water, the Spirit of the Lord caught away Philip, that the eunuch saw him no more: and he went on his way rejoicing.

What can a deacon learn from this account of Philip that will help him to be a caring witness?

Philip was attentive to the voice of the Lord. "And he arose and went." When the angel of the Lord spoke to Philip, he was willing to go, even though the exact purpose and location were not clear. The caring witness is ready to respond immediately to the voice of God when he speaks.

Philip was willing to get involved personally. Instead of holding back, not wishing to get involved, Philip responded immediately when "the Spirit said unto Philip, Go near and join thyself to this chariot. And Philip ran thither to him."

Philip knew the Scriptures and was able to interpret God's plan to the eunuch. Philip was familiar with the Scriptures and used his knowledge to enlighten the eunuch regarding God's plan for sending the Messiah. Philip led the eunuch to the Lord and baptized him.

Yes, Philip baptized the eunuch. You, as a deacon, can perform any spiritual service that your pastor can perform if authorized by the congregation. Your only limitation is in the performance of a marriage ceremony. And this hurdle is a matter of legal relationship with the state.

The world calls out today for deacons to "go ye" as caring witnesses. Thank God for deacons who, like

Philip, have heard and obeyed Christ's command "Go ye."

"Becoming" Deacons Possess a Spiritual Glow

Stephen, like Philip, was one of "the seven" who served ably in the early Jerusalem church. He had helped to heal the break in the fellowship. He and the other six men had served well. Acts 6 records that the word of God continued to increase after their work was completed. Soon Stephen was to give his life as the first martyr for Christ. Acts 6:8 says, "And Stephen, full of faith and power, did great wonders and miracles among the people."

His witness soon drew opposition. He was taken before the council. False witnesses spoke against him. But we see something of Stephen's Christian witness even while on trial. "And they were not able to resist the wisdom and the spirit by which he spake. . . . And all that sat in the council, looking steadfastly on him, saw his face as it had been the face of an angel" (Acts 6:10,15).

What a testimony of faith! Mr. Deacon, as you go about your work, does your Christian spirit glow? Can others see Christ in you? Are you the caring witness God wants you to be—and you desire to be?

Become a Caring Witness

Early Christians won the pagan to Christ by demonstrating a loving, glowing, Christlike spirit. Early Christians lived out their religious experience in daily life. Christ was real to them. These early Christians shared their love with others.

As a deacon, launch out into the deep. Become a fisher of men. Don't wade in the shallows of spiritual experience. Become a caring witness. As a deacon, you will have frequent opportunity for sharing your faith as you visit in the homes, offices, or hospitals as a part of your deacon visitation.

What are the characteristics of the caring witness?

A caring witness has an abiding spiritual interest in people. His concern is more than a legalistic interest. He's not concerned with people for what they can do for him. A caring witness is willing to be a friend. He will take the time required to cultivate a trusting friendship.

An article appeared in *The Deacon*, written by an alcoholic who told of his encounter with Charlie _____, a Baptist deacon. The writer told how he had drifted from job to job and problem to problem. He said, "Charlie continued to call and counsel with me. He always let me know that the people of Watertower Church were praying for me. I'd like to be able to say that 'once upon a time there was an alcoholic who accepted Christ and was able to stay sober from that day on.' However, we all know that stories that begin with 'once upon a time' are fairy tales.

"It was three months after I became employed at a local hotel that I hit 'the skids' again. Only this time Charlie was there to catch me. He and his wife, Ann, took me to live with them. Their homelife was an inspiration to me. The closeness of Charlie's family and the devotion of God was not something they dragged out of the closet on Sunday and paraded to church. Charlie lived, ate, and slept his religion. He was constantly involved in ministering—whether to Widow Jones, whose stove was not adjusted properly, or to the lost in our community. His phone rang constantly at suppertime. His answer was always, yes. He told me that he received more enjoyment out of helping people than they did in being helped. He loved to tell people what Christ had done for him—how through the help of a concerned Christian, he was led to receive Christ as his Savior. He never became impatient when the people he was working with would 'turn him off.' Charlie, the deacon, was a caring witness."

A caring witness shows empathetic concern. Empathy is that quality that allows you to identify with others. An empathetic person has the ability to put himself in another person's place. Empathy is the ability to walk in someone else's shoes. Empathy allows you to feel emotionally as another person does. Your capacity for empathy can grow as you work with people and show honest concern for them.

I recall visiting in the home of one of the church families assigned to me as a deacon. Visiting with me that night was a fellow deacon who had recently lost his wife. He and I were going to visit the home of a church member whose wife had just died. As we entered the front door of the home, the grieving husband who had just lost his wife, put his arm around my fellow deacon. "I am so glad you came! You are the only one who can understand my heartache." They both knew the pain and loneliness of losing a wife.

Quietly they supported each other in a tearful embrace.

You can develop an empathetic spirit. You do not have to experience every sorrow that others know. But empathy grows out of a spirit of love, compassion, and respect for others. Empathy comes to the one who is willing to bear the pain of another and try to help him carry the personal load of grief.

A caring witness has a personal concern for lost people. Our modern world has sought to smooth over words like "lost" and "sin." A caring witness, however, must have a deep concern for the lostness of persons without Christ and, like Philip and Stephen, witness a glowing Christian faith.

Opportunities abound for the caring witness. People surround you who need your Christian support. I think of the persons I know who need a friend. There is Bill. He is a young adult caught up in the pressures of today's young business executive. He has three children at home. His wife has been in a mental institution three times. It appears that medication will relieve her problems only temporarily. The young man already has developed a problem with alcohol. He seeks to be a concerned husband and a loving father. But the pressures of his work and the long absences of his wife are crashing in on him. He feels that he is without a friend. He experiences heavy guilt for not spending more time with the children. He is a lonely, hurting, face in the crowd—needing Christ and Christian friends.

Then there is Frank. I met Frank about two years ago in a state government building when he was working as a prisoner. Frank is fifty-four years old. He has spent twenty-eight of these years in various state prisons. His family has disowned him. His term will keep him behind the walls for the remainder of his life. He has tried to escape on three occasions but has been caught each time. He is hungry for friends and relationships. He now serves as a trusty and says that he has accepted Christ. How do you help a lonely, hurting man like Frank?

Robert Murray McCheyne, longtime Scottish pastor, found the secret for helping persons like Bill and Frank during his years of ministry. McCheyne's church sexton (custodian) of many years gave the answer when he was once asked by a church visitor to explain the glowing power of Pastor McCheyne's preaching and ministry. The old sexton seated the visitor at the desk where his pastor had prepared his sermons. Then he said to the visitor: "Now put your elbows on the desk. Put your face in your hands. Now let the tears flow. That's the way Brother McCheyne used to do."

6
Support Your Church and Denomination

Now that you are a deacon, you will want to develop a better understanding of your church and denomination. Support grows out of understanding and appreciation. As a deacon, you will have frequent occasions to draw on a working knowledge of your church and your denomination. In turn, you will be able to help others develop a foundation for understanding. A deacon needs to know the history, doctrines, and relationships of his church and denomination in order to function more effectively.

More than one hundred years ago the French political scientist Alexis de Tocqueville visited America. He traveled extensively, seeking to discover the dynamic of this country and its people. Reflecting on his American travel experience he said: "I saw the genius and greatness of America in her commodious harbors and her ample rivers, and it was not there; in her fertile fields and boundless prairies, and it was not there; in her rich mines and her vast world of commerce, and it was not there. Not until I went to the churches of America and heard her pulpits aflame with righteousness did I understand the secret of her power."

Would de Tocqueville be able to make this same

observation today if he could visit churches of America again? Does the spirit of righteousness permeate your church and community? As a deacon, you have a place of Christian service where you can set aflame the spiritual ministry of your church. Just think of the impact that deacons could have across America if church by church could be touched by a revival of righteousness. Do you know the foundational nature and purpose of your church? Do you understand the reason Christ entrusted his spiritual mission to the churches?

The Church Is Divine in Nature

Each time I drive past a certain stone church building near my home I am impressed by an attractive sign out front. The sign reads:

The ＿＿＿ Church

Gathers Regularly in This Building

The sign calls to the attention of all who pass that this church is comprised of the people of God rather than being a building constructed of stone and mortar.

Recently a fire destroyed a large church building in a suburban area of Nashville. A local television station showed on the evening news dramatic pictures of the devastating fire. The dollar loss was staggering. As the fire burned out of control, a television newsman interviewed one of the church leaders. The announcer said, "I know that the loss of your total church must be a tragic shock to you!" In a calm reply the church member said: "Yes, it is a shattering tragedy to lose our building. But you must remember that our church did not burn. Only our church building was destroyed. Our church is made up of God's people. I am sure that we will worship together next Sunday some place in the community."

What a testimony on the nature of the church!

Christ established the church—and he is the head of the church. Just as God established the family as a part of his divine plan for grouping units of society, so God gave the church as a divine plan for maintaining the spiritual welfare of mankind. Jesus said, "Upon this rock I will build my church" (Matt. 16:18). Note his personal involvement: "*I* will build *my* church."

During his earthly ministry Jesus laid the foundation for his church. He knew that it would continue his work after he returned to the Father. When Jesus and his disciples met for worship, fellowship, teaching, or ministry, the embryonic church was in evidence. Jesus spoke lovingly of the church as he taught his disciples or spoke to the multitudes. He referred to the spiritual vitality of the church by saying, "The gates of hell shall not prevail against it" (Matt. 16:18).

The forces of evil lash out at the church because it represents Christ and his divine mission on earth. Early in the ministry of the first church in Jerusalem this fellowship of the redeemed was rocked by "mummering." The Holy Spirit led in the selection of men of spiritual maturity to bring healing to the fellowship. Pastor and deacons have labored together through the centuries as men of God dedicated to strengthening the spiritual ministry of God's church.

Until Christ's return, deacons should stand firm in

loyal and dedicated service directed toward the advancement of the church. Christ is still head of the church. Rejoice that you have a place of ministry and service in his church. We see Christ's love for the church in its scriptural description. The church is described as the people of God, bride of Christ, and temple of God. As a gathered people—a called-out people—let us follow Christ in support of his church.

The Church Has a Divine Purpose

A Baptist church is made up of redeemed persons who have experienced spiritual conversion and have been baptized as a symbol of their conversion from sin to life. The converted person has a new spiritual nature. He is a new creature in Christ. Christians will desire to meet regularly with other redeemed persons for worship and fellowship. Joining together for nurture and spiritual growth is essential for a Christian.

As Jesus looked out over Jerusalem and wept because the people were lost, as a sheep without a shepherd, so Jesus gave an imperative to his followers: "Go therefore and make disciples of all nations, baptizing them in the name of the Father and of the Son and of the Holy Spirit, teaching them to observe all that I have commanded you" (Matt. 28:19-20, RSV).

Through the years this portion of Christ's purpose for his church has been called the Great Commission. His purpose is for the redeemed to "Go ye" as ambassadors for him. Christians have no choice. The church is to be a going army, seeking out the lost. Church members are to make disciples of all nations. Christ said dramatically that all persons are to be reached with his message of salvation. His authority is given to his followers. Converts are to be baptized as a symbol of their newness. His church is to be a teaching and training fellowship, always interested in providing loving nurture to those who have accepted him. The Great Commission ends with a comforting acknowledgment, "And lo, I am with you always, even to the close of the age" (RSV).

The Church Has Divine Functions to Perform

Just as the body has basic systems that must be performed if life is to continue, so the church has vital spiritual functions that must be kept alive and healthy. As the body has primary functional systems, such as circulatory, respiratory, and nervous, so the church has basic functional systems.

You will be enriched in your understanding of your church if you are aware of these primary systems, or functions. Your body cannot continue to perform when these major functions weaken and cease operation. Neither can a church maintain its spiritual nature and purpose if its primary spiritual functions fail. Paul spoke of the total body functioning together in Christ when he said, "From whom the whole body fitly joined together and compacted by that which every joint supplieth, according to the effectual working in the measure of every part, maketh increase of the body unto the edifying of itself in love (Eph. 4:16).

What are these basic spiritual functions of the church that are so vital to continuing life support?

1. Worship

If God's people who comprise the fellowship of a church fail to maintain the function of worship, the church will eventually weaken and die. A fellowship of the redeemed must gather individually and corporately. Christians must experience an awareness of God and respond to him in obedient reverence and service. A church must experience the abiding presence of God in their midst. Worship is enhanced through prayer, Scripture reading, testimony, giving, and joyous celebration in musical praise. Thanksgiving and adoration flow upward to God to energize a people at worship.

Deacons have a strategic role in building the true spirit of worship in their church. Deacons lead out in setting the worship tone as persons who participate in worship leadership. Deacons serve with the pastor in leading public prayer and Scripture reading. The Lord's Supper provides opportunity for worshiping God through a divinely established ordinance of spiritual remembrance, dedication, and fellowship. Baptism is an ordinance of deep spiritual meaning in which deacons and their wives often provide a leadership role. Deacons serve alongside the pastor in enriching the worship experience so that fellow Christians rejoice together.

2. Proclaim the gospel

Proclamation of the gospel message is central throughout the New Testament. Jesus taught his disciples repeatedly that his message of salvation should be central in their lives. "Go ye" is a theme of much that Jesus taught. Stephen and Philip, members of "the seven" in the Jerusalem church were powerful witnesses. Stephen became the first recorded martyr. What a heritage Stephen and Philip gave to today's deacon.

Deacons are charged with the responsibility to be proclaimers for God. As a deacon, you have so many opportunities for proclamation. You can proclaim by the example of daily life and involvement in personal witnessing. Proclamation is not an elective for the deacon; it is a requirement.

3. Educate

A church must be a body that continually learns more about God's special nature and purpose. A growing, vibrant, healthy church is one that keeps the Bible open and is taught regularly. Mature Christians seek to involve themselves in training activities that will help them become more effective in his service. Remember Jesus commanded Christians to "Go ye . . . teaching them to observe all things whatsoever I have commanded you" (Matt. 28:19-20).

A strength of Baptist churches has been their Bible teaching program. The largest school in the world is the church Bible school, manned by volunteer workers who love the Lord. The Bible has been the chief curriculum for churches that are growing. Teaching and training are essentials for every church.

Deacons should be joyful participants in their church training program. A learning deacon is a growing deacon. A growing deacon is an involved deacon—involved in learning about Christ and, in turn, involved in teaching and training others to learn and to grow.

4. Ministry

Another basic function of a living, growing, vibrant church is ministry. People are hurting. Great personal needs exist. Jesus went about ministering to the needs of persons. Human needs must often be met before there is opportunity for spiritual ministry. We are to minister in Christ's name. Our loving response is to be made because Christ first loved us.

Ministry is at the heart of the deacon's work. As a co-laborer with the pastor, today's deacon ministers in Christ's name. The Deacon Family Ministry Plan is designed to give deacons an opportunity to minister to a small portion of the entire flock. The deacon becomes the undershepherd, working side by side with his pastor.

Understand Baptist Polity

Baptists believe that each congregation has authority to govern itself with each member following the leadership of the Holy Spirit in all matters. As a self-governing congregation, each church then is responsible for determining its own objectives, goals, program, organization, and leaders. Each member is dependent on himself, with God's strength, but each church is also interdependent on the fellowship of churches of similar belief. Church business is conducted by each congregation according to policies and procedures each church establishes. Specific guidelines are established by each church to determine how work is to be carried out in harmony within the congregation.

The *Broadman Church Manual* declares: "Persons participating in congregational decisions bear a heavy responsibility. Each person is, of course, free to express his personal opinion during discussion. But each member should remember that he is to seek his own understanding in light of the Holy Spirit's leadership. Opinions expressed in congregational business meetings should be expressions bathed in the spirit of patience in Christ in love. . . . Churches following true congregational polity do not send *delegates* to associations, state Baptist conventions, or Southern Baptist Convention meetings. Neither does a church hold formal membership in these equally autonomous groups. Church members are appointed by the church to attend meetings of these separate groups. These *messengers* vote as individuals not as *delegates* representing the church."

Understanding How Baptist Churches Organize

Each Baptist church organizes its work as it desires in order to achieve its basic purposes most effectively. True, a Baptist church is a divinely appointed organism. But it also has dimensions of organization in that it must group certain portions of its work together and delegate responsibility to organization structure and human leaders. These organizations and leaders are commissioned by the congregation in business session and, therefore, are responsible to the congregation for performance. These organizational leaders report back to the church in regular business sessions.

Even though each church may organize to meet its

own needs, there is considerable unity in patterns that Baptist churches follow. There are variations but the following organizational approach is used by a majority of churches.

Pastor and deacons—these leaders serve as co-laborers in proclaiming the gospel to believers and unbelievers; providing care to persons in Christ's name; providing leadership in assisting the church to attain its objectives; and building and maintaining church fellowship.

Church officers and committees—serve to implement work for the congregation that would be difficult for the entire congregation to perform as a corporate body. Examples of administrative-type officers and committees are: clerk, treasurer, properties committee, nominating committee, finance committee. Program service leaders are elected to direct essential support services, such as church library and church recreation services.

Church program organizations—these serve as educational-type organizations that have a membership, content, and regular times for membership meetings. Examples of church program organizations are: Sunday School; Church Training; Missions (men, women, boys, girls); Church Music.

Understand What Baptists Believe

Paul set forth high qualifications for the deacon in 1 Timothy 3. Several of these qualifications speak of the deacon's knowledge and Christian conviction.

Paul saw the deacon as one possessed of Christian purpose, a holder of the Christian faith, tested and proved, and bold in the faith. He obviously believed that a deacon should know sound doctrine. A deacon was to know what he believed about his Christian faith.

What do Baptists believe? As a deacon, can you talk intelligently about basic Baptist principles?

As a part of the 150th anniversary celebration of the organization of the first Baptist national organization in America, a group of eighteen Baptist leaders and scholars developed a statement of *Baptist Ideals.* Although individual Baptists may express themselves differently on some doctrines, these excerpts from the statement of *Baptist Ideals* provide a brief and worthy statement of basic doctrinal beliefs.

I. AUTHORITY

1. Christ as Lord

The ultimate source of authority is Jesus Christ the Lord, and every area of life is to be subject to his lordship.

2. The Scriptures

The Bible as the inspired revelation of God's will and way, made full and complete in the life and teachings of Christ, is our authoritative rule of faith and practice.

3. The Holy Spirit

The Holy Spirit is God actively revealing himself and his will to man. He therefore interprets and confirms the voice of divine authority.

II. THE INDIVIDUAL

1. His Worth

Every individual is created in the image of God and therefore merits respect and consideration as a person of infinite dignity and worth.

2. His Competence

Each person is competent under God to make his own moral and religious decisions and is responsible to God in all matters of moral and religious duty.

3. His Freedom

Every person is free under God in all matters of conscience and has the right to embrace or reject religion and to witness to his religious beliefs, always with proper regard for the rights of other persons.

III. THE CHRISTIAN LIFE

1. Salvation by Grace

Salvation from sin is the free gift of God through Jesus Christ, conditioned only upon trust in and commitment to Christ the Lord.

2. The Demands of Discipleship

The demands of Christian discipleship, based on the recognition of the lordship of Christ, relate to the whole of life and call for full obedience and complete devotion.

3. The Priesthood of the Believer

Each Christian, having direct access to God through Christ, is his own priest and is also under obligation to become a priest for Christ in behalf of other persons.

4. The Christian and His Home

The home is basic in God's purpose for human well-being, and the development of Christian family life should be a supreme concern of all believers in Christ.

5. The Christian as a Citizen

The Christian is a citizen of two worlds—the kingdom of God and the state—and should be obedient to the law of the land as well as to the higher law of God.

IV. THE CHURCH

1. Its Nature

The church, in its inclusive sense, is the fellowship of persons redeemed by Christ and made one in the family of God. The church, in its local sense, is a fellowship of baptized believers, voluntarily banded together for worship, nurture, and service.

2. Its Membership

Membership in a church is a privilege properly extended only to regenerated persons who voluntarily accept baptism and commit themselves to faithful discipleship in the body of Christ.

3. Its Ordinances

Baptism and the Lord's Supper, the two ordinances of the church, are symbolic of redemption, but their observance involves spiritual realities in personal Christian experience.

4. Its Government

A church is an autonomous body, subject only to Christ, its head. Its democratic government, properly, reflects the equality and responsibility of believers under the lordship of Christ.

5. Its Relation to the State

Church and state are both ordained of God and are answerable to him. They should remain separate, but they are under the obligation of mutual recognition and reinforcement as each seek to fulfil its divine function.

6. Its Relation to the World

The church is to be responsibly in the world; its mission is to the world; but its character and ministry are not to be of the world.

Understand Your Baptist Origins

In 1607, the same year that Jamestown was being established in what is now the state of Virginia, a significant event in Baptist history took place. Two Englishmen, John Smyth and Thomas Helwys took a small group of Separatists from England to Holland. The Separatists were persons who formed their own congregations because they felt the Church of England was following Roman Catholic practices too closely. Smyth and Helwys believed that the New Testament proposed believer's baptism and not infant baptism. Later some of the Separatists returned to England with Thomas Helwys and began a church near London. This church was begun in 1612 and is believed to be the first Baptist church in England.

Another leader in the English Baptist cause was William Carey. Trained as a shoemaker, he became the father of the modern missionary movement. Known around the Christian world, Carey brought attention to the Baptist cause. Carey served forty years as a missionary in India, beginning in 1793.

In America Roger Williams formed the first Baptist church at Providence, Rhode Island. This church was formed in the late 1630's. Roger Williams had been a Separatist in England. Other prominent Baptist names in early America were John Clarke and Elias Keach. Clarke was both a medical doctor and a preacher. Keach was a major force in the establishment of the first association of Baptists in Philadelphia. For forty-four years the Philadelphia Association was the only Baptist association in America.

The first Baptist church to be established in the South was the First Baptist Church, Charleston, South Carolina. It was begun about 1696.

Other prominent Baptists during early years in America were Adoniram Judson and Luther Rice. Both men were Congregational missionaries—but became Baptists. Rice returned home from the mission field and gave his full time to preaching and gathering financial resources to enable Judson to continue his missionary work in Burma. Rice was the leader in establishing a Baptist national organization in 1814. This first national organization was usually called the Triennial Convention, and its major purpose was to support the expansion of missionary work.

In 1845 the Southern Baptist Convention was organized in a meeting held at First Baptist Church, Augusta, Georgia, with 300 persons present from 165

churches. In this first meeting, the Convention established a foreign mission board and a home mission
board.

Baptists Around the World

In 1905 the Baptist World Alliance was organized
to provide communication, fellowship, and channels
to meet special needs. The Alliance is composed of
the various Baptist groups around the world. The Baptist World Alliance does not provide any kind of organic
structure. Its basic purpose is to facilitate fellowship
and sharing of mutual strength and assistance. Every
five years the Alliance has a congress to bring together
messengers from a fellowship of approximately
28,000,000 Baptists in 97 conventions and unions in
76 countries around the world. In all, there are
32,000,000 Baptists in 130 countries. Most Baptist
groups in North America cooperate with the North
American Baptist Fellowship, which functions within
the framework of the Baptist World Alliance.

How Baptists Organize Work and Relationships

As you can readily see by the large number of Baptist
bodies around the world, there are various organizational approaches and relationships within these
bodies. Since congregational government is the basic
polity of Baptists, there are many similarities to approach in organization and relationships.

As a deacon, you need to be aware of how your
denomination is organized and operates. My own denomination is Southern Baptist. Using the Southern

Baptist Convention as a model, I will demonstrate the general organization approach used by some major bodies. Terminology will be different but basic organizational structure has more similarity than dissimilarity among Baptists. Each church is an autonomous body. Under the leadership of the Holy Spirit each church sets its own programs and goals. The churches, working together in fellowship, establish general bodies that assist in performing corporate work that the individual churches could not achieve. Southern Baptist churches follow an organization system that is comprised of churches, associations, state conventions, and the Southern Baptist Convention. As mentioned earlier, there is a worldwide fellowship of Baptists through the Baptist World Alliance.

Messengers are elected by each church to attend the meetings of associations, state conventions, and the Southern Baptist Convention. There is significance in our use of the term "messenger" rather than "delegate." The persons elected by a local congregation to attend the association, state convention, or Southern Baptist Convention are not instructed as delegates by the church regarding how they should vote. Messengers from the churches make up the assembly of the specific denominational meeting.

James L. Sullivan, former pastor and president of The Sunday School Board of the Southern Baptist Convention, says in *Rope of Sand with Strength of Steel:* "There are no inferior or superior bodies in Baptist life. The association, state convention, and Southern Baptist Convention are all on the same level. The major differences are in geographical location, size of annual meeting, and nature of the work undertaken. All work together for the same objectives under this polity. Associations are not added up together to make the state convention, neither are the state conventions added together to make up the Southern Baptist Convention. Rather, each is an entity within itself. Each is an autonomous body making its own decisions and living with them responsibly.

"Sometimes the term 'denomination' and 'convention' are used interchangeably. This is not correct usage." Sullivan says, "The denomination is much larger than the convention. Although the convention is made up of the messengers sent directly from the churches to annual meetings, its major ongoing work is carried on between annual sessions. Their work is done by agencies through delegated responsibilities. The denomination is made up not only of the Southern Baptist Convention but of nearly three dozen state conventions, almost 1,200 associations, more than 34,000 cooperating churches, and about 12 and a half million believers."

The Executive Committee of the Southern Baptist Convention serves as the general coordinating body for the denomination between annual business sessions. It has no direct authority or control over the various agencies. The Executive Committee has responsibility for functions such as acting in an advisory capacity between different agencies, recommending an annual budget to the Convention, and general publicity and promotion of the Convention's work in cooperation with the other agencies. Members of the Executive Committee are elected at the Southern Baptist Convention annual meeting.

Four different boards have responsibility delegated to them by the Southern Baptist Convention.

Foreign Mission Board
Home Mission Board
Sunday School Board
Annuity Board

In addition there are several Commissions and Institutions responsible for specific areas of assignment such as Brotherhood Commission, Christian Life Commission, Education Commission, Historical Commission, Radio and Television Commission, Stewardship Commission, Southern Baptist Foundation, and six Seminaries.

7
Grow as a Christian Steward

Now that you are a deacon, you will want to grow as a Christian steward.

The Christian realizes that possessions are only temporary. The day will inevitably come when you must leave your money and other tangible possessions.

Albert McClellen says in *Christian Stewardship:* "God holds original title to all created things, and while he might temporarily relinquish ownership to man, there is a reversionary provision that in the end all things will still belong to him."

There is nothing evil in the acquisition of wealth. Daily living requires man to labor in order to provide the essentials for existence. Money is not the root of all evil as some incorrectly say. What Paul actually said was "For the *love* of money is the root of all evil: which while some coveted after, they have erred from the faith, and pierced themselves through with many sorrows" (1 Tim. 6:10, italics added).

As a deacon you will want to examine your own life to be certain that your material possessions are placed in proper priority. Your life needs to show that you believe all possessions belong to God. You are only a steward or trustee of these gifts. A Christian, out of love and thankfulness, should regularly give a portion of personal possessions back to Christ—through his church.

Stewardship Covers All of Life

People often think of "money" when the word stewardship is mentioned. But there are other significant personal possessions besides money. In fact, money is only a by-product. Money usually comes as a result of your investment of time and talent—both God given.

Let's take a look at these elements of stewardship and see how they apply to you—now that you are a deacon.

1. Invest Your Time and Talent

Time is an ultimate human possession. There is something awesome about watching grains of sand sift quickly through an hourglass. Fleeting sand reminds us of fleeting time.

As a deacon, you need always to be aware of how you program the priorities of your life. Time is a diminishing resource that can easily slip through your fingers.

What concerns should you, a deacon, have for proper investment of your time? Where does Christ fit into your priorities?

How can you invest your time for Christian purposes? Obviously, through participation in your church.

The happy, joyful, productive deacon is one who is personally involved in the life and works of his church. He attends regularly, along with his fellow Christians, because he finds spiritual fulfillment in worshipping God with others.

I know a physician whose churchmanship always encourages me. His medical practice is consuming. But my friend, a deacon, programs his personal schedule so that he is always at church on Sunday morning and evening—except when an absolute emergency intervenes. He serves as director of a senior adult department. One of the department members, who rides a church bus from her retirement complex each Sunday often tells me that "Dr. _____ rode the church bus today to pick us up." This means that he must arrive at least one hour ahead of the Sunday School starting time in order to ride the bus to meet his elderly members. He has found the joy of investing his time in Christian service.

Recently I was talking with a college professor—a deacon. He spends many hours each week visiting for his church. When I asked about his time schedule he replied, "The Lord has been so good to me. I am nearing retirement age and still have my health. I promised the Lord that I would give him as much time as possible in my remaining years."

I think of another friend who retired four years ago. He had managed a multimillion-dollar business for over twenty years. Prior to his retirement he told me of his plans to serve as a volunteer education director and administrator in a small Baptist church. He has followed through with his dream. He and the church have been blessed.

Last week I talked with a deacon in a distant state who is a successful accountant and business consultant.

Feeling that God gave him his talent for business, he has tried to invest his time and talents in the Lord's work. He works with Baptist churches to establish sound financial policies and practices. He told me, "By giving my time and skill to churches that need help, I feel like I am making some contribution with the gifts God gave me."

Another deacon friend is a dentist with a flourishing practice. For the past several years he has invested one month each year to serve without pay on a foreign or home mission field. He practices dentistry for Christ. He told me once, "I just wish I could really tell you what the Lord has done for me during these mission experiences. I get far more than I give."

These men are investing their time, talent, and money for the Lord—and enjoying every moment of their stewardship.

An article in *The Deacon* told of an elderly deacon who has invested his time and talent in his church. A veteran Mississippi deacon, E. E. Tate, received a certificate from his church in recognition of "faithful service to the church, exercise of talents for the house of God, and giving without hope of recovery."

The article stated: "Believing that a new church should have new furniture, he started to work in his shop and made a communion table. Then he built a matching pulpit, pulpit chairs, choir chairs, and tables for the church. All these furnishings are still used today.

"He even made the church's communion trays. One pastor requested that Tate make a set of dual-purpose plates to allow serving of both the bread and the cup at the same time. This service is now used exclusively during the church's Lord's Supper services. Friends and associates readily admit that E. E. Tate is a deacon who has a great love for his church—a love that has grown through the years as he has advanced in age, matured in faith, and grown in grace."

Thank God for deacons like E. E. Tate. There are legions like him who are happy stewards of their time and talents.

2. *Invest Your Influence*

As an exemplar leader, a deacon should be a steward of his influence. "Be thou an example" said Paul.

I was talking with a young operator of a service station recently. I have known him since he was a teenager working at his father's service station. His father has two brothers who also own service stations in the same town. We talked about the abundant training the young man had received from his father and uncles—and how their training had helped him. He said: "One of the best lessons I learned was from my dad. He occasionally reminded me that our family name was known for hard work, honesty, and dependability. Dad would say, 'Son, I am depending on you to uphold the family name.' " The father, a solid churchman had been a lasting influence on his son.

Marse Grant, a veteran state Baptist paper editor, once told me about a deacon in North Carolina. Living on a rural farm, the deacon had a favorite place to pray in a wooded area near the house. He would kneel to pray in the same place each time. Getting up from his prayer, he would always pick up a small stone and toss it in front of him. In time, the pile of rocks grew into a large mound. After the devout deacon died, his children took the stones and built a monument in his memory.

His Christian influence lives on in his children and friends.

Several years ago most state Baptist papers carried an article written by a veteran airline pilot—a faithful Baptist deacon. Deeply concerned about a difficult problem, he felt that he had to speak out against the growing practice of serving liquor to airline passengers during flight. Though a career pilot with a major airline, this quiet, unassuming deacon finally had to declare his convictions. He wrote: "Drinking in airplanes creates nuisances and embarrassment as well as actual danger for the pilot, the stewardess, and the passengers. The biggest danger is from the passenger who has been drinking before boarding, and who drinks enough on the flight to make him intoxicated."

He told of a drunk passenger trying to kick and force the exit door open while the plane was flying at 8,000 feet—insisting all the time that the plane was not in the air. The pilot knew the danger to every passenger.

Here was a deacon who was not afraid to speak out. His influence was felt across the nation. A congressman saw the article and personally read it before the Congress—and then requested that it be printed in the *Congressional Record.*

L. O. Griffith, pastor and denominational leader, related an experience he had with a deacon that demonstrates the power of personal influence. "A deacon vigorously opposed a mission project that was presented to the church. He threatened to stop giving if the church voted against him. His pledge was 30 percent of the church budget. The church voted, however, in favor of starting the mission.

"The deacon took a walk—but not to church. He would walk to the town bank about once a week to pay on the church note for a building debt. He would not pay through the church. After some time, it was rumored that the deacon was coming back to church. His place as Sunday School director had not been filled. One Sunday morning the deacon returned.

"He asked for a general assembly of the Sunday School. He walked to the pulpit with his hat in his hand. As he approached the pulpit he put on his hat, a gesture very much out of character with him. Taking off his hat as he stood before the assembled Sunday School, he said, 'My hat is off to you for what you've done while I've been gone. I didn't think you could do it without me.'

"Taking his coat off, he pitched it over a chair and said, 'My hat is off to you, and now my coat is off with you. I'll never take another walk—except *for* the church.'"

The people knew the man loved the Lord, loved people, loved his church, and loved his pastor. The deacon had been brought up in an anti-missionary community. He explained that he had not realized the importance of starting a new mission—but now he realized that he had been wrong.

As a deacon, he had been effective before. Now his new spirit and commitment made him able to bear more abundant fruit. His Christian influence made an impact during his remaining years.

3. *Your Money*

Paul started one of the qualifications of a deacon as being "not guilty of greedy lucre" (see 1 Tim. 3:8). A deacon's spirit should exemplify a wholesome concern for stewardship. He knows that all he possesses comes from God and desires to share his worldly goods for the advancement of Christ's work.

John Claypool, Baptist pastor, gave this insight on the subject of the tithe in a sermon on the meaning of money: "The principle of the tithe was born in an agricultural setting. It was soon realized that if there was going to be another crop, some of this year's harvest had to be saved for seed. If everything were eaten, that is, if all were taken out and nothing put back into the cycle, the whole process would collapse. The tithe was "the seed fund," as it is a principle that applies to all of life. If you are not putting at least 10 percent of what comes in to you back into the process of life, you are a taker, a freeloader, a burden in the process of creativity."

Money represents the fruit of man's labor. A deacon should be a cheerful giver of tithes and offering.

There are three areas related to money that should concern a deacon.

1. How money is gotten

The way his money is earned should be of importance

to a deacon. Money that is gained improperly or illegally is out of character with both the biblical qualifications and spiritual ministry of today's deacon. Many Baptist churches have written or adopted statements of church covenant that speak to a Christian's business involvement.

Money secured in shady business deals, usurous interest rates, or at the expense of the impoverished is not in keeping with the high spiritual standards that should be held by a deacon.

2. *How money is spent*

Charles Smith raises a strange question in his refreshing book *How to Talk to God When You Aren't Feeling Religious*. If Jesus were living today "would he drive a Cadillac or a Volkswagen?" After the initial shock of so impertinent a question, the subject has food for thought.

How would Jesus view today's materialistic way of life? What methods would he use to communicate his message if he were living on earth today as he did centuries ago? What would be his teachings regarding personal possessions?

These questions must be faced by today's deacon if he is to determine his own position as a Christian leader.

A stewardship book with a contemporary flair for word usage is titled *Bread*. Its subtitle is "Living With It/Making It/Sharing It." In one chapter the author explores three warnings about "bread" (the name given *money* by our younger generation, if you aren't hep to the language).

"Don't let your bread become an idol.

"Don't hoard bread.

"Don't let your bread take on ultimate value."

A deacon should have great concern that his approach to stewardship is consistent with the Bible's teachings. Paul taught: "For everything created by God is good" (1 Tim. 4:4, RSV). We are caretakers of our material possessions. Money can be good, if used wisely by a steward. Or money can be bad, if used selfishly by the one who possesses it for a season.

Claypool says: "Tithing can be misused. For example it can become legalistic or mechanized when a person gives 10 percent of his income, grudgingly or without love. Tithing can also produce a false sense of security. Some people seem to have no love for Christ but are proud of the money they give to their church. We need to remember that God and his love are not for sale. To think that we own stock in God because we give a tithe through the church reflects poor thinking. Tithing can put a limit on our giving. Ten percent is only a suggested amount. There may be people who can afford to give more."

3. How money is left after you are gone

Your Christian influence can live on in your estate after you are gone.

Have you ever wished that you were able to give more to the financial support of your church and denomination? A Christian should be concerned with how his money is used after his death. Your objectives and goals can live on through your legal will. In fact, some persons have been able to give larger amounts to Christian causes after their death than during their life.

Several years ago Baptist Press released this news account regarding a Madison, New Jersey, deacon who went on ministering after his death. The news release said:

Part of a $175,000 estate belonging to a Negro Baptist deacon here was left to the Madison Baptist Church, affiliated with the Southern Baptist Convention.

"The first we knew about it was when a rather gruff voice asked over the telephone, 'What is the name of your church?' " said Howard Hovde, pastor of the Madison church.

"When told it was the Madison Baptist Church, we were informed the church had been included in the will of John J. Yancey, a deacon emeritus of the First Baptist Church of Madison," he added.

Since the First Baptist Church is affiliated with the National (Negro) Baptist Convention and Yancey was a Negro, Hovde thought a mistake had been made.

"But, in fact, both churches had been included as beneficiaries," he added. "The Southern Baptist church is one of 22 beneficiaries of the will.

"Actually, it was at Madison that the first prayer group of Southern Baptists met which started work in eastern New York. Manhattan became the center of the work, but 2½ years ago the group from Madison again began to meet there to avoid the long trips into New York City.

"The unusual gift from Mr. Yancey will assist our church toward the goal of $100,000. We will ever be grateful to him for his kindness," Hovde said.

Your legal will can provide you a way to keep on giving to God's work through your church or denomination.

Paul expressed his stewardship desire for the Christians in the church of Macedonia, "Now I want you to be leaders also in the spirit of cheerful giving" (2

Cor. 8:7, TLB).[1] Deacons could well make this their prayer regarding their own stewardship.

The legendary editor, William Allen White, once presented some land for a park to Emporia, Kansas. When asked why he gave the land he replied, "This is the last kick in a fist full of dollars that I am giving away today. I have always tried to teach that there are three kicks in every dollar: one when you make it, another when you save it, the third when you give it—I get the biggest kick of all in this last one."

Understand Church and Denomination Financial Plans

A deacon needs to understand his church and denominational financial plans. He needs this knowledge to better appreciate how his tithes and offerings are used in Christ's work around the world. He also needs this knowledge so that he can better interpret the drama of God's work to persons whom he meets in his deacon ministry.

Most denominations have a financial plan that enables the churches to minister corporately.

In my own denomination, we have a corporate financial plan called the Cooperative Program. I will use the Cooperative Program of the Southern Baptist Convention to illustrate one plan used by a denomination to finance a wide range of ministries around the world.

Early Days of the Cooperative Program

Southern Baptists searched for a plan for securing

[1] *The Living Bible, Paraphrased* (Wheaton: Tyndale House Publishers, 1971). Used by permission.

and disbursing funds from 1845 until 1925. But an acceptable plan was elusive. Seeking to find a financial plan for corporate work, without sacrificing the principle of church autonomy, was difficult.

Both foreign and home mission work were approved in 1845 at the first meeting of the Southern Baptist Convention. Missions have always been the heartbeat of most Baptist churches and denominations. Without a total plan for financing denominational efforts, each mission agency was forced to employ field representatives to travel extensively seeking funds. It sometimes required more than half the money collected to pay the salaries and expenses of these field representatives.

In 1925, the Southern Baptist Convention established the Cooperative Program—a total denominational plan for financing joint work.

How the Cooperative Program Works

The following interpretation of the Cooperative Program was presented recently in a Church Training publication, *Source.* "The Cooperative Program is a joint enterprise of the state conventions and the Southern Baptist Convention through which churches carry out their worldwide program. Each convention plans its own program, yet all work together. Each state convention adopts a Cooperative Program budget with a chosen percentage going to the Southern Baptist Convention. In turn, the Southern Baptist Convention adopts a budget built on the anticipated receipts through the states.

"The percentage of Cooperative Program gifts sent from the states varies from 25 percent to 50 percent with 35 percent being the average. Churches are asked to make one Cooperative Program allocation. Their gifts are sent to the state convention and there divided between the state and the Southern Baptist Convention.

"The individual member is linked through the church to the whole Baptist enterprise. The plan depends on responsible stewardship by all—the individual, the church, and the conventions. Failure at any point would hurt the plan.

"The Cooperative Program does work. It goes as far as the generosity of Baptists allow it to go. For example, in the United States it helps make possible 67 colleges with 97,000 students, 34 child-care homes with 5,500 children, 38 hospitals ministering to 10,000 patients daily. In other countries it provides Baptist schooling for 73,483 students and hospital care for 948,329 patients annually. It has helped establish 14,001 churches and missions in 76 countries where 57,366 converts were baptized in 1972."

8
Magnify Christ in Your Home

Now that you are a deacon, Christ should be preeminent in your home.

God established both the family and the church. The family is the primary structure that holds the fabric of society together. The church is the spiritual body that nurtures the Christian and proclaims God's message to the unbeliever.

The home and the church have some similar characteristics. Unity and love should abound in each. Strong bonds of fellowship should hold the members together. Paul even referred to the church as the "household of God" (1 Tim. 3:15).

The church is described as the body of Christ. Christ is the head. The church is a living, vibrant, spiritual organism. As a deacon, you now have the opportunity to show the glowing dimension that Christ brings to a family.

Paul recognized that the deacon's family life was a witness for both the home and the church. He stressed the kind of father and husband the deacon was to be. Paul also laid down spiritual qualifications for the deacon's wife.

Even the casual observer of family life can see that

the forces of evil are crashing in on both the home and the church. Just as you, a deacon, have responsibility for building and maintaining church fellowship so you have responsibility for enriching your own family life.

A View of Family Life Today

Joe W. Hinkle, denominational family ministry leader, quoted the following statistics regarding family life in America today.

"Between one-third and one-fourth of all marriages end in divorce. Four out of ten marriages end in divorce by the end of the seventh year. One child out of every six children will live in a one-parent family before their eighteenth birthday. One in nine families are headed by a woman—sometimes living under the national poverty level. Maternal desertion seems to be a phenomenon of today. Refusal of either parent to accept custody of the children upon divorce strikes fear in the hearts of children."

Someone has said that marriage is an art, but too many people are treating it as unskilled labor. The situation is truly critical. The time is late.

But deacons can make an impact through their ministry of spiritual support and care. Your Family Ministry Plan work carries you into the homes of families that may have already cut out on the church. And the parents may be seriously considering cutting out on each other and the children.

Now that you are a deacon, there is great work for you to perform in family ministry.

The Bible Speaks on Deacon Family Life

What does the Bible have to say about the deacon's family life? How do these admonitions relate to today's deacon?

Paul realized that a family needed a leader. He had much to say about the role of the father as spiritual leader. Christian teaching should begin in the home by precept and example—led by the father.

Study the qualifications that the Bible sets forth for the deacon and his wife.

". . . husband of one wife . . ."

God's message through the centuries has resounded: "Thou shalt have no other God before me." A person should give firm allegiance to one God. In like manner, Paul says that the deacon should give his loving allegiance to one woman. Paul did not mean that an unmarried man was unqualified to serve as a deacon by saying a deacon should be the "husband of one wife."

Keep in mind the setting of Paul's day. Just as the pagan turned to several gods—so the pagan often had several wives. Women were looked upon as property to be owned. But Christianity brought a new value system to human life and relationships.

The deacon was watched constantly by the pagan. His life was examined. Paul, therefore, was indicating that the deacon should be an example in marriage.

Robert Hastings, quoting a distinguished university president, said in *How to Live with Yourself:* "The most important thing a father can do for his children is to love their mother. A giving love, that is. A sharing love. A love that brings fulfillment to each. A love that makes room for individual differences. A love that sheds light and warmth to all who come under its spell, whether it be the couple's own children, their friends, or other loved ones."

". . . ruling their children and their own houses well . . ."

A deacon's family was to be a model of Christian love and productive personal relations. As a father, the deacon should provide parental direction and nurture.

I mentioned earlier that a favorite hobby for our family is organic gardening. We recently added a beehive to provide pollination for the garden and honey for our kitchen table. To watch a colony of bees at work provides some insight into human family dynamics. Every bee has a distinctive job to perform. Worker bees labor daily making a foundation wax comb for storage of the honey they produce. Immature bees, themselves not yet able to fly, feed the younger bees. A queen bee repopulates the hive. Guard bees are stationed near the entrance to drive away any intruder. On a cool day the bees heat the hive. On a hot day they cool the hive. Together the colony of bees work as a productive team.

Today's deacon should strive to lead his family to work together in harmony with a Christian father providing loving, participative leadership.

David and Virginia Edens in *Why God Gave Children Parents* reports the answer a thirteen-year-old boy gave to the question, "What do you think makes a happy family?" He summed up his answer in these words: "A happy family reminds me of a baseball team with Mom pitching, Dad catching, the kids fielding, and with everyone taking a turn at bat." The authors added: "A Christian home is where persons live a shared life, where decisions are made by consensus of the whole family. Every member has something to contribute."

A deacon's Christian spirit should light the way for such a family relationship. His family should be able to see Christ living and working through the Father.

Qualifications for the Deacon's Wife

What does the Bible say about the deacon's wife?

". . . Be grave . . ."

The word *grave* sometimes gives the impression that Paul meant a deacon's wife should appear somber or melancholy. Actually, the word denotes a spirit of worship or reverence. A deacon's wife is to be one who worships God and possesses a reverence for holy things. Her faith gives her an inner resource. She renews her strength through her daily walk with the Lord.

Once while visiting an Oklahoma town I saw a statue to "The Pioneer Woman." It was erected in tribute to the determined frontier women who helped settle the West. The sculptor had captured her strength of soul and body. In one hand she held a Bible. With her other hand she held onto a small child. Upon seeing the statue I recalled what someone had said about a mother. "One good mother is worth a hundred schoolteachers and an ounce of a mother is worth a pound of parson."

Paul knew the influence of a Christian woman in the deacon's home when he wrote about the deacon and his wife.

Kearnie Keegan once told me of the memorial service in Formosa for Inabelle Coleman, longtime missionary. The service was conducted by several of those persons she had won to Christ. High government officials were present. The university faculty was represented. A Chinese man read a brief history of Miss Coleman's life in Chinese. When he concluded, he said in English, "For those who did not know Miss Coleman, no words are adequate to describe her life. For those who knew her, no words are necessary."

". . . *not a slanderer* . . ."

The ability to keep confidences is of crucial importance to the deacon's wife. She will often have access to delicate information regarding persons in the church. She may know information that could affect the life and work of the church. She must constantly resist the temptation to gossip.

Paul stated that the deacon should "not be double-tongued." He is to be a man of his word. Truth and integrity are to characterize him. Both the deacon and his wife are to be consistent in their conversation and relations with others. They were not to talk cream and live skimmed milk, as Dwight L. Moody used to say.

". . . *sober* . . ."

A deacon's wife is to demonstrate a balance and

temperateness in all of life. Even though the wife of early deacons lived in a world characterized by indulgence, she was to live a disciplined life.

"*. . . faithful in all things . . .*"

Few more positive affirmations could be given to a deacon's wife today than to say that she was faithful in all things.

Sure, there will come difficult and tiring days as she goes about her daily life. A deacon's wife is human and heir to all the emotional stresses of her peers. But her Christian character gives her capacity to bear the load.

I recall an incident shared by a summer conference speaker concerning a wife who had been keeping her three young children inside the home on a cold rainy day. Everything that could go wrong had gone wrong. To prepare her husband for her dark mood she pinned a short warning note to the front screen door. "Worn Threadbare . . . Will Ravel!"

Yes, of course, those moods do come. But the busy, productive, happy days far outweigh them.

What can the deacon and his wife do to magnify Christ in their home? How may they serve together in partnership as deacon and wife.

Here are some practical suggestions:

- Let the joys of Christian family living be demonstrated in your family.
- Be supportive of your church through personal leadership and regular attendance at worship

services, prayer meetings, and teaching/training activities.

- Practice family worship in your home.
- Be concerned for the needs of families about you.
- Share in the joys of deacon service together.
- Provide affirmation and support to pastor, staff, fellow deacons, and their families.
- Pray together that you and your family may be caring.

Now that you are a deacon, you have great work to do!

9
Know the How and Why of Deacon Work

Through the years as I have participated in deacon conferences across the nation, certain questions are always asked. Here is a list of these questions and my response to them.

Question: **Why are deacons ordained? And does this ordination give deacons any special authority or power?**

Answer: When "the seven" were first chosen to help solve a potential break in the fellowship of the Jerusalem church, Acts 6:6 states, "And when they had prayed, they laid their hands on them." These early Christians followed an ancient Jewish tradition of placing their hands on the head of the person being honored.

No special power nor authority results from the ordination of deacons. Ordination is a meaningful act of Christian fellowship which, in essence, says to the new deacon being ordained: "We believe in you and have confidence in your spiritual maturity. We will pray for you and give you our support as you minister among our fellowship."

Q: **What is deacon rotation? And what are the benefits of rotation of deacon service?**

A: Most Baptist churches follow a plan of deacon rotation. A deacon is usually elected for a term of three years. At the end of three years' service, each deacon rotates off the deacon body and is not eligible for re-election for at least one year. At the end of one year the deacon again becomes eligible for election by the church.

Rotation makes it possible for more persons to serve as deacons. There are numerous qualified young adults, for example, who could serve as a deacon if elected. Fresh and enriching ideas result from new members joining the deacon body. Rotation also helps prevent the establishment of a "board of deacons" over a period of years as the same persons serve term after term.

The phrase "once a deacon, always a deacon" is sometimes heard. This phrase refers to the fact that the spiritually mature deacon will continue to maintain his spiritual vitality whether he is officially serving on the deacon body or not. When a deacon joins another church, however, he must be elected by that church before he can serve as a deacon in that church.

Q: **What is the best way to elect deacons?**

A: Election of church leaders must always remain a responsibility of the church. Church members vote on the election of deacons just as they vote to call a new pastor. There are many different patterns by which names of prospective deacons are submitted to the church for election. Each church must determine the plan that seems best for them. Some churches present the names of all adult male members except those who have requested that their name not be submitted, plus those persons who have just rotated off the deacon body. Other churches use the church nominating committee or special deacon selection committee to select names to be presented to the church. When the deacon selection committee plan is used to present names, usually several more names are presented than are to be elected. For more specific details see *Broadman Church Manual* or *The Ministry of the Deacon*.

Q: **What is the relation of church committees to deacon committees? Do church committees report to the deacons?**

A: Church committees, such as finance, properties, and nominating committees are elected by the church to provide specialized services for the congregation. As church committees they report to the church. From time to time a church committee may share a report with the deacons for informational purposes. Church committees report to the church in business sessions and do not need approval by the deacons before presentation to the church.

Deacon committees, on the other hand, are selected and elected by the deacons to perform special deacon responsibilities. Examples of deacon committees are Lord's Supper, baptism, and ushers. Deacon wives often serve on the baptism committee to assist female members prepare for the ordinance of baptism.

Q: **Does the pastor supervise the deacons or do the deacons supervise the pastor?**

A: Both pastor and deacons are elected by the church. Deacons do not supervise the pastor, nor does the pastor supervise the deacons. As co-laborers in ministry, pastor and deacons share in proclaiming the gospel, caring for persons in Christ's name, and building Christian fellowship. Both should support the other with love and openness of spirit. Deacons report directly to the church on their work. Churches have found it a good practice to elect a church personnel committee to work with the pastor in establishing policies regarding work of church staff personnel. The pastor should supervise the work of church staff members. As a church staff grows, care should be exercised to group similar jobs and delegate supervision of staff to certain strategic staff members, such as the minister of education.

Q: Why isn't the title "board of deacons" used today as widely as it was once used?

A: "Board of deacons" is an unfortunate term that is foreign to decision-making in a church governed by congregational polity. The term crept into Baptist usage and was used rather widely in years past. A "board" is usually a group of leaders who make basic decisions. In a Baptist church there is no person or group that makes final decisions for the congregation. Baptist polity allows each member to vote on business matters as the Holy Spirit gives insight. As deacons have moved into the area of ministry alongside their pastor, the term "board of deacons" is heard far less. Most churches refer to these co-workers as the deacons, deacon body, or deacon group.

Q: Should a church have junior deacons?

A: Some years ago there was considerable use of junior deacons. In a majority of churches that elected junior deacons, there was usually a body of senior deacons who operated in areas of administration, often as a board of deacons. In an effort to get pastoral ministry work achieved, junior deacons were elected since the senior deacons usually continued in church management work. As senior deacons died or rotated off the deacon body, they were usually replaced by men who had served as junior deacons and who were committed to the deacon ministry of proclaiming, caring, and building fellowship.

There is a growing practice of coupling a younger man with a deacon for training in ministry. The younger man takes part in deacon training projects, in visitation with an assigned deacon, and in deacon meetings in a non-voting capacity. Various titles are given to these plans, such as Yokefellow or Deacon Partner Plan.

Q: What is the relation of the church council's work to the deacon's work?

A: The purpose of the church council is to plan, coordinate, and evaluate the total church program. The pastor usually serves as chairman of the church council, whose membership is comprised of the heads of all church program organizations, program services, and strategic church committees. The chairman of deacons serves as a member of the church council. It is important to remember that the church council is not an administrative type committee but rather an advisory and correlating type. Since the church council is elected by the church, it reports to the church. Implementation of church council plans is carried out by the appropriate church organization or committee.

The deacons, on the other hand, have a different type ministry than the church council. Deacons have responsibility for personal involvement in activities of personal witnessing, Christian caring, and church fellowship.

Q: Should a church elect deaconesses?

A: Bible scholars give different interpretations as to whether there were deaconesses in the early New Testament churches.

Ray Summers, veteran Baptist seminary and university professor, spoke to this question in an article that appeared in most state Baptist papers. Excerpts from his article states: "The Greek word *diakonos* may be either masculine or feminine as many English words may be, such as servant, person, singer, student.

"In Romans 16:1 Paul commended Phoebe to his readers. He called her a *diakonos* of the church at Cenchreae. He urged his readers to receive her in the manner appropriate for God's people and to give to her any help she might need because she had helped many others including Paul.

"Revised Standard Version translates the references to Phoebe 'deaconess.' *The Living Bible, Paraphrased* uses 'dear Christian woman.'

"*The New English Bible* translates 'a fellow Christian who holds office in the church.' *Today's English Version* says "our sister, Phoebe, who serves the church.

"Did Paul mean that she was deaconess in the sense of an officer in the church? It is possible that he so used it. The degree of probability of his so using it is greatly debated."

Women are equipped by temperament to serve in pastoral ministry activities. A significant number of churches in the American Baptist Convention have elected deaconesses. Only a very few Southern Baptist churches have elected women to serve as deacons. In view, however, of the unparallelled service opportunities in the mission action program of Woman's Missionary Union, most churches have seen small need for electing deaconesses today. To do so might add overlapping organizational structure that could lead to an actual decrease in service."

Q: What deacon officers should be elected? How should deacons organize to perform pastoral ministry work?

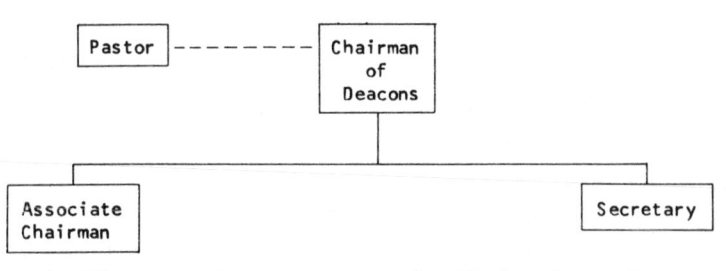

A: The organization pictured calls for three deacon officers: chairman of deacons, associate chairman, and secretary. The chairman of deacons should work closely with the pastor. His major responsibilities as chairman are: (1) leading the deacons to plan and conduct their assigned work; (2) direct the Deacon Family Ministry Plan, an organized ministry to church families; (3) plan and coordinate deacon training projects; and (4) serve as a member of the church council.

The associate chairman's responsibilities are: (1) assuming leadership of the deacon body in absence of the chairman; (2) coordinating the preparation for the ordinances of the Lord's Supper and baptism; and (3) assisting the chairman in special projects as needed. Many deacon bodies are electing the associate chairman with a view to his becoming chairman at the end of one year. Such a practice provides continuity of leadership and enables each deacon chairman to have practical knowledge of the work.

The deacon secretary is responsible for (1) keeping accurate records; (2) preparing reports and official correspondence of deacon work; and (3) securing required deacon literature and resources.

In larger churches which desire to expand the ministry of the deacons, four other officers are often elected. These are the proclamation leader, community relations leader, family care leader, and the fellowship leader.

Q: **How does a church go about selecting a new pastor when the pastor resigns? Are the deacons involved?**

A: Following established church procedures, a congregation, in business session, should elect a representative Pastor Selection Committee to locate, interview, and recommend a qualified minister to serve as pastor. Since the church elects the members of the Pastor Selection Committee, the committee should report directly to the church.

The Pastor Selection Committee membership should be representative of the entire church. Some committee members may be deacons. But their election should result from their ability to represent the church well in this important assignment rather than because they are deacons.

Q: Can you sum up briefly the spirit, work, and relationships of a deacon?

A: The best summary statement that I have seen was written by Garland Hendricks, veteran pastor and seminary professor. The statement appeared in *Church Administration* magazine under the title "A Deacon's Code of Ethics."

I am a deacon in a Baptist church. In Christ I am saved from sin to a life of faith and usefulness.

In the church, of which Christ is head, I have an opportunity to make my life count for him in Christian service.

The members of my church have expressed confidence in me by making me a deacon.

By the grace of God, in keeping with the mind and purpose of my Lord, and in response to the confidence of my brothers and sisters, I herby commit myself to—

THE BIBLE

I accept the New Testament as my source of authority on the Christian life and the work of a deacon. From it I learn that deacons were first chosen to serve with the pastor in the ministries of the church, that they were ordained by the church to serve people in need, that they were expected to set an example in Christian life and service.

Proper Authority

The church determines my specific authority, and I will be true to its constitutional or special instructions to its deacons.

The Lord Jesus Christ has granted me spiritual authority, and I will be true to him by setting a Christian example in everyday living.

My conscience, quickened by the Holy Spirit, gives moral authority; and I will strive to be wise, fair, loving, and courageous in dealing with current issues.

The Pastor

I am my pastor's partner and co-worker. Both of us are responsible to Christ, and we are co-workers for Christ.

My pastor is shepherd of the flock, and I will strive to help him be a good shepherd by:

Praying for him

Encouraging him

Defending him when he is criticized unfairly

Being frank with him when I think he is mistaken

Being his brother in Christ, his co-laborer in the church, and his moral and spiritual helper in service to people.

Other Deacons

I recognize that I am engaged in teamwork with my pastor and the other deacons. I will:

Respect the other deacons

Pray for them

Strive to understand their points of view when we do not agree and will disagree in love

Carry my share of responsibility at all times

Defend them if they are attacked or misunderstood by others.

The Church

I will strive to work responsibly with all who are members

of the church by:

Attending the services and participating in the work of the church

Supporting the financial program of the church

Encouraging the indifferent members and praising the faithful ones.

Supporting the decisions of the church even when I am in the minority

Discouraging envy, jealousy, backbiting, and strife

Refraining from gossip and insisting that the truth be told about all matters

Guarding sacredly any confidence entrusted to me

Bearing witness to the unsaved and appealing to them to accept Christ and join the church.

My Lord

Of myself I am neither wise, good, nor strong enough to be a deacon. But I am not alone in this work. Christ is my companion, and through his wisdom, mercy and power I am able to serve.

LIST OF RESOURCES

Although deacons are elected to their office because they have proved themselves as worthy of special responsibility, they would be the first to admit that they need help in learning their tasks. These resources will promote growth.

The Ministry of the Deacon, Howard B. Foshee (revised December, 1974.)—This popular book has been revised to include latest information on deacon ministry in the church. The book helps deacons know what their responsibilities are and how to perform them. It presents deacon history and explores the changing role of deacons today. The book suggests ways deacons may organize and do their work and outlines procedures for electing, ordaining, and rotating deacons. (Convention Press)

The Ministry of the Deacon (gift edition).—A handsome hardbound gift edition of the book described above, plus a Presentation Certificate in the front of the book. Although designed primarily for deacon's ordination, it may also be used at other times when the church or a friend wants to do something special for deacons. (Convention Press)

The Ministry of the Deacon Study Guide.—This book is designed to reinforce personal study of *The Ministry of the Deacon.* The workbook includes learning activities for both group and individual study. (Convention Press)

The Deacon Tapes, Charles Treadway and Howard B. Foshee.—Three cassette tapes are included in a vinyl case with a four-page study guide for each tape. Deacons may use the tapes in a study group or in individual study experiences. (Broadman Press)

On Being a Deacon's Wife, Martha Nelson.—Suggestions are given to deacons' wives to enrich their lives. The author encourages deacons' wives to learn more about their husbands' service as deacons and to find ways to support their ministry. (Broadman Press)

Handbook for Deacon Chairman.—This booklet contains practical guidelines for the deacon chairman to use in planning, conducting, and evaluating deacon work. (Broadman Press)

Deacon Family Ministry Plan Resource Book.—Designed to provide deacons with all the basic resources needed. A 6- by 9-inch three-ring vinyl notebook with the following items included: *Deacon Family Ministry Plan* program help booklet, 15 Deacon Family Information Forms, 12 Deacon Family Ministry Calendar Forms, 12 Deacon Family Ministry Report Forms, 15 Deacon Family Referral Forms, Deacon Family Ministry Orientation Leaflet, *The Ministry of the Deacon*, and six colored tab dividers. (Convention Press)

The Deacon Family Ministry Plan.—A filmstrip designed to introduce deacons to the Deacon Family Ministry Plan. It's purpose is to define the Deacon Family Ministry Plan, to illustrate how it works, and to inspire deacons to consider implementing the spiritual ministry. 50 frames, color, manual, and recording. (Broadman Press)

Ministry of the Deacon Today.—A filmstrip designed to train deacons and to interpret the work of the deacon to the congregation. Qualifications for deacon service, the task of the deacon, and organization to perform these tasks are discussed. 50 frames, color, manual, recording. (Broadman Press)

Broadman Church Manual, Howard B. Foshee.—This small hardbound book will help deacons understand Baptist church programs, organization, polity, and church relationships. (Broadman Press)

Called to Joy: A Design for Pastoral Ministries, Ernest E. Mosley.—A guidebook for deacons, pastors, and church staff members to lead their church in pastoral ministries. Written in laymen's language, the book is designed to help leaders and churches of all sizes. (Convention Press)

Pastor Appreciation Day Kit.—This kit is designed for deacons to use in planning a Pastor Appreciation Day. The kit includes one booklet, two posters, one button, and a certificate. (Convention Press)

Growing a Loving Church, Bob Dale.—This book is designed to help pastors and deacons achieve maximum efficiency in growing a loving church by updating their caring skills and learning new approaches to helping people. (Convention Press)

Vocational Guidance in a Church, Francis A. Martin, Alice S. Magill, Ernest E. Mosley.—This book serves as a practical resource in guiding the reader to help others achieve self-understanding, choose a vocation, and find fulfillment in their work. (Convention Press)

When Trouble Comes, John Ishee, compiler.—The case studies in this book cover a spectrum of personal and family problems. Helpful insight and information for dealing with these problems are given. (Broadman Press)

Proclaim the Gospel: A Guide to Biblical Preaching, Alton H. McEachern.—This book is designed to provide basic helps on biblical preaching and worship leadership. (Convention Press)

Don't Sit on the Bed, William G. Justice.—A handbook of practical suggestions for hospital and nursing home visitation. This book gives counsel for making visits a helpful experience for the patient and for yourself. (Broadman Press)

The Baptist Deacon, Robert E. Naylor.—This book by the president of Southwestern Baptist Theological Seminary has long been a best seller. (Broadman Press)

"The Up Side of Down".—A sixteen-page booklet with envelope to be given or mailed to hospital patients. (Broadman Press)

Facing Grief and Death, William P. Tuck.—This book offers help for the grieving and for those who would comfort them. It provides both practical and inspirational counsel for facing death and bereavement.

(The resources listed above are available in your Baptist Book Store.)

The Deacon. —This magazine is prepared especially for deacons. Each quarterly issue contains success stories, how-to stories, picture stories, feature stories concerning deacon ministry, guidance for deacon officers, and resource material for conducting deacon meetings.

The Deacon Family Ministry Plan. —This is a twenty-four page booklet which offers training for deacons in family ministry. It gives practical approaches for involving deacons in a meaningful family ministry.

(The two resources listed above are available from Materials Services Department, 127 Ninth Avenue North, Nashville, Tennessee.)